Communicating With The Other Side

Communicating with The Other Side

True Experiences of a Psychic-Medium

Betsey Lewis

I've had the privilege of knowing two amazing psychics in my life — Armand Marcotte and Betsey Lewis. Both Armand and Betsey have touched lives with their remarkable gift of prophecy. — Ann Druffel, bestselling author of *The Psychic and the Detective* and *Past Lives, Future Growth*

Communicating With The Other Side: True Experiences of a Psychic-Medium
By Betsey Lewis

© 2014 by Betsey Lewis. All rights reserved.

Reprint June 2015

ISBN-13:978-1499365894

ISBN-10:1499365896

No part of this book may be reproduced, stored in a retrieval system or transmitted by means without permission of the author.

Cover design by Dragonfly Dimension Design

Dragonfly Dimensions Publishing (S), Boise, Idaho 83709

www.dragonflydimensionspublishing.com

Contact: info@dragonflydimensionspublishing.com

Dedication

In memory of Kathy, Bette, Fred, Moe and Joe—forever in my heart.

A special thanks to my husband, Rick, and my beautiful Spirit Friends and Guides for always having my back and inspiring me to write this book.

I'm truly blessed!

Contents

Introduction	11
One: In the Beginning	23
Two: Saving Kathy	35
Three: A Guy Named Joe	39
Four: The Signs are Everywhere	53
Five: Spirit Steps In	65
Six: A Journey Ends	79
Seven: Remote Viewing	89
Eight: Reincarnation is Real	93
Nine: A Volcano Dream	101
Ten: Crossing Over	107
Eleven: Learning Indigenous Ways	131
Twelve: S.O.S. From Spirit	147
Thirteen: Kathy's Validations	157
Fourteen: Premonitions	163
Fifteen: Client Readings	167
Sixteen: Answers from Spirit	179
Seventeen: Kathy's Big Surprise	213
Epilogue	217
About the Author	225

Introduction

Before you begin reading this book, I'd like to make it perfectly clear this is a memoir about the spiritual and paranormal events that have changed my life and brought me a greater understanding of the Other Side after the deaths of close family members. It's not about the clients I've read for, although I've included a few readings in the book—it's about life, death and the beautiful confirmations from my departed family and the remarkable warnings and premonitions given to me by my spirit guides through the years.

So I must reiterate, if you are looking for a book about a medium who talks to spirits all day long—and there's some excellent books out there, then this book isn't for you. The supernatural began for me at 8-months of age and continues today. I call myself a psychic-medium because I see future events before they happen as well as communicate with spirits on the Other Side. I'm clairaudient which means I can hear voices from the Other Side. I'm clairsentient which means I can read people, and I'm clairvoyant and have the ability to see the future and events before they happen. Most mediums receive only impressions from the departed people, but not global premonitions as I've experienced since childhood.

My immediate family—my first husband, my parents, my stepfather and my sister have all passed, and I feel blessed that they returned to validate life continues on. Sometime in your life you will experience a loved one's death, and for each of us, death is personal. How will you react from a death in your family—tears, sorrow, depression, anger, guilt? Most of us will feel profound guilt that we weren't there when our family member passed or expressed our love for them, or perhaps apologized for some argument or hurt. I experienced all those emotions and learned great lessons from my family, and by telling my story, my wish to you is that when death rocks your world, you will find comfort that death is just another door we pass through on our cosmic evolutionary journey.

My first experience with the spiritual world began at the age of three when I had a clear awareness of the existence of other beings and other dimensions beyond everyday physical reality. Although I don't recall my two invisible spirit guides, my parents said I provided detailed descriptions of them and claimed they gave me important messages. My next supernatural event happened at age eight after my paternal grandfather passed away and he stood beside my bed late one night. The experience was so frightening, I asked him to never appear in spirit form again, and he never did. Spirit now comes to me usually as audible voices. I've become clairaudient.

My very first supernatural event happened at the age of eight months old. My parents were attending the University of Idaho in Moscow and decided to drive to Twin Falls in the southern part of the state on a weekend. My father had driven the road many times and new it would take eight hours to arrive in Twin Falls. But something happened that night as they drove through the New Meadows area, dotted with a few ranches. I was snuggled inside a wicker basket on the back seat. There had been no cars on the highway that night which my parents thought was odd. Suddenly a horrendous roar descended on the car, shaking it violently as if a plane was about to crash on them or near them. My father slammed on the brakes, got out of the car and scanned the sky. The roar stopped and there was nothing in the sky—nothing to explain what had frightened them moments before.

The strangest part about the terrifying experience came to light thirty years later when my uncle related the story and recalled how my parents couldn't account for two hours missing hours—a scenario that reminded him of the famous Betty and Barney Hill ET abduction in 1960 where the couple lost several hours in time on a lonely New Hampshire road. Under hypnosis Betty and Barney recalled they had been abducted by extraterrestrials and given a physical examination.

Due to my uncle's stunning revelation in 1981, I began contacting people who used regressive hypnosis. My first call was to the late Budd Hopkins, renowned alien abduction investigator and author. He suggested I contact MUFON (Mutual UFO Network) in Los Angeles where I lived at the time. Days later, I received a call from MUFON investigator and author Ann Druffel, one of the foremost investigators of alien abduction who had already written a book on the subject—*The Tujunga Canyon Contacts*. In September of 1981 Ann hypnotized my mother first, taking her back to that night, and a few months later, I was regressed. Our sessions didn't prove conclusively that we were abducted by aliens, but it did prove that something strange happened that night. The entire sessions are included in my book, *Angels, Aliens and Prophecy II*.

A poll recently taken indicates that millions of people believe that they've been abducted by other worldly beings. I've always sensed our world contains layers of realities and beings unseen to us. My second UFO encounter took place while I walked home from first grade. Soon after this event, I began to have recurring dreams of catastrophic Earth changes, which I believe are accelerating now. I continue to have those precognitive dreams of earthquakes and volcanic eruptions.

My first encounter with a spirit apparition took place after my beloved paternal grandfather passed away suddenly from a massive heart attack in 1958. I prayed he'd contact me again from the Other Side, and he did, but it proved to be a frightening experience to see a gauzy-white apparition of a man standing beside my bed in the middle of the night. By age eleven, I began reading for family and close friends, and continued through the years, although not professionally. Life's unforeseen events made it impossible to provide full time readings. Only eleven years ago I began to provide astrological and psychic-medium readings for an international clientele.

Here's how the book came about. My dear younger sister

Kathy left the physical world on July 19, 2003, which had been our father's birth date. Shortly after her death she began contacting me from the Other Side, but then the activity suddenly stopped. She began her communication again on July 9, 2013, Thanksgiving 2013, and through the 2014-2015 holidays. At first the spirit activity began with a newly purchased stereo-radio shutting off whenever my husband and I turned on the Kool Oldies FM radio station in the morning. We tried to rationalize the paranormal events taking place in our house as the paranormal activity continued each morning at precisely 6:50 am and 7:10 am. We discovered the radio had a built-in timer, and thought this explained the events. Boy, were we wrong! We cleared the timer on the radio every day, but the activity continued, plus more strange anomalies took place through the months.

How do I know it was Kathy? The first time the radio shut off by itself, the sixties song *Cathy's Clown* by the Every Brothers played, a song she had loved. It also shut off whenever we mentioned her name or whenever I walked into the kitchen. As time went by other anomalies began to manifest—kitchen utensils floated off the counter and into the sink, my husband felt someone touching his head in the middle of the night, and our cat Comet freaked out in the hallway by Kathy's photograph on the wall. There was much more to come.

How could a new stereo purchased four months earlier, that had worked perfectly, suddenly turn itself off almost daily and at specific times? My thought was her visits were to warn us of a family member's passing, which has happened to me in the past. But soon I realized that she was on a mission. Dreams and psychic impressions indicated she wanted me to write another book about my spiritual experiences. I was supposed to write about my paranormal/spiritual experiences; something I had planned to do years before. One thing I know for sure is that Kathy maintains her sense of humor on the Other Side.

Through the years I've had the honor of reading for clients in South Africa, Sweden, Australia and a large portion the United States, but after my first nationwide interview on Coast to Coast AM with George Noory on November of 2013 and on Ground Zero everything changed. Suddenly I was overwhelmed with requests for psychic readings worldwide—and I was touched by such beautiful requests.

I've received such extraordinary validations from spirit over and over through the years, for friends, family members and clients, and this confirms the importance of my psychic gift. Spirit always surprises me with messages and insights needed for each personal reading. But there was a point during my teen years that I honestly wished I didn't have the gift of prophecy, because of persistent visions of three high school classmates dying in car accidents. All three classmates, including my best friend, Nancy Mayer, tragically died in separate car crashes, just as I had envisioned. These fatal car crashes were caused by drinking and driving, and could have been avoided.

At that point I questioned why I'd been shown such dreadful things if I couldn't change the outcome. I felt such guilt, sorrow and helplessness. I regretted that I didn't warn my classmates of my visions, but then I wondered if warning them might create the event. Through the years I've learned that each one of us decided on a spiritual road map before we entered into our physical bodies, and we decided on the way we'll leave our physical bodies. We can deviate from our original life plan, make some changes for the better, and sometimes for the worst—and that's called free will. Our life had a road map to follow which we agreed upon before we entered this world. Of course, we had guidance from our spirit guides and angels.

After the deaths of my classmates, I decided, "Enough! No more visions!" I didn't want to see these horrible events, and so I suppressed my psychic ability for many years. But spirit wasn't going to let me be an ostrich, and hide my psychic head in the sand for long. Nope, the messages and visions soon returned, with incredible clarity.

I think we've all asked what exists beyond death. In this book, I answer questions such as does love transcend physical death? Do our loved ones watch over us and reach beyond the veil of death to communicate with us from time to time? Can we learn to communicate with them? What is the soul? Are humans the only ones who possess souls? Do our pets have souls, and do they reincarnate? Who are the "new" children, and what is their mission on our planet? What are orbs? No matter how evil a person has been, can their soul make amends? Do we go to a heaven if we have lived a righteous life, or to a hell if we've lived a horrible life, full of hate, violence and anger, according to Christian teachings?

Most of all, we want to know if our loved ones are happy and at peace on the Other Side. From countless precognitive dreams and paranormal experiences, as well as from insights from my spirit guides, I've glimpsed what awaits us when we finally pass through that mysterious door called Death, and have included questions and answers in this book. I certainly don't have all the answers about the Other Side, but I do have a real sense of what awaits us. It's beautiful, wonderful, joyful and pure love. The Other Side is more real than your physical existence on Earth, and more alive, you might say. We are endless, like the cosmos, and forever evolving.

We are conditioned to believe nothing exists beyond our five senses—sight, smell, touch, taste, and hearing, and yet the majority of us have discovered there is much more than our five senses. We all possess what is known as a 'sixth sense', that tells us when something isn't quite right. Countless stories can attest to people experiencing warnings that have saved their lives or the intervention of deceased family members or spirit guides/guardian angels, who step in to help them in their time of need.

In school I was taught that one of the most basic laws of science is the Law of the Conservation of Energy. Energy cannot be created or destroyed; it can only be changed from one form to another. We humans are definitely energy, and after our physical bodies die, our consciousness is free to explore other dimensions. The "soul and mind" are ubiquitous, existing in many dimensions at once.

For ages indigenous cultures have communicated with their deceased ancestors in sacred ceremony, believing their ancestors still reside close by but unseen. Spirit resides not only in our ancient ancestors but within everything on Mother Earth—the wind, the air, the mountains, the water, fire, as well as in Earth's animals—the winged, the four-legged, and the sea creatures. Indigenous peoples have always known that nothing dies, it only transforms from one state of energy into another.

Spirit has always been part of my life. I know without a doubt that the world of spirit is extraordinary. Our loved ones are always near us, to guide and comfort us through our earthly sojourn, long after they have departed. How can we believe that once we've passed over to the Other Side we'd forget about family and friends, and no longer have any earthly concerns? I know that I'd never desert my family and my love after I've gone on to the Other Side.

Spirit has touched my life in so many ways; I can't begin to tell you. Spirit continues to communicate with me, through whispers, dreams and telepathic communications, and every day I give thanks for this divine gift. There are skeptics, and that's fine. Psychics and mediums can't be one-hundred percent accurate each and every time. Even mediums and psychics like Edgar Cayce, Theresa Caputo, John Edwards, and Patrick Mathews have their off days. Unfortunately, there are frauds in every kind of business that prey on gullible people and charge exorbitant fees for their services. That's despicable. Sadly, people seek readings because they are desperate for answers, and believe that psychics are all-seeing and all-knowing, when, in fact, psychics are fallible humans. Psychics make mistakes because every human on this planet has the gift of free will and change their destiny through manifestation.

My mission is to help people find their true mission in life, and validate a loved one's presence. Most people don't realize they were born with special talents and gifts, and sometimes they let those talents lay dormant most of their lives. If people knew their divine path, they'd live much happier and joyful lives.

Of course, there are people I refer to as "spiritual couch potatoes," those souls who really don't want to do much in their present life, and that's fine. Everyone has free will to do and explore and learn whatever they want in each lifetime. But I must caution those who do this that in a future incarnation they will need to make up for their laziness as "spiritual couch potatoes."

My greatest frustrations are people who don't live up to their potential God-given talents because they think it's too late to pursue their dreams. I see what talents and abilities we brought into the world through individual personalized astrological chart and soul path information I provide with each reading. Sadly, a great number of people don't honor their talents. Another interesting observation I've made is that people don't act on what spirit conveys to them through me. They continue in the same rut they've created for years, and complain that life won't give them a fair shake. Ridiculous! Destiny doesn't control us, we control destiny.

You see, I learned long ago that our thoughts are powerful, so powerful that they influence our future. If we focus on our difficulties, hardships and fears, we stay in a holding pattern, and fail to experience our full potential as spiritual beings. There are no coincidences in life—each person we meet in life touches us in ways we may never fully understand at the time. Spirit provides a divine path for each of us, and guides us into learn powerful lessons through the people we encounter.

In *Communicating with the Other Side*, I've included a few readings provided for my clients through the years, without using real names, to protect their identity and maintain their privacy. Although I'm a medium, spirit doesn't always come through each and every time for a client, so I rely on my psychic gifts, which has proven to be quite remarkable.

Recently I received this email from Rosemary in Hawaii. "I felt immediately at ease connecting with Betsey. It actually was very refreshing. I got re-inspired to complete some things (very near and dear to my heart) that I have put on the back burner. Additionally, I felt I got to reconnect with a sister again. There were many blessings in this session." This is just one of many beautiful emails I've received, and I'm honored and blessed to help such wonderful people worldwide.

Read on and discover how spirit has blessed my life, and hopefully will bless your life with the knowledge that Love lives on Forever.

Chapter One
In the Beginning

I arrived on planet Earth at 7:48 in the morning, on the 7th day of March, weighing in at 7 pounds, in Moscow, Idaho, to my parents, Bette and Fred, who were attending the University of Idaho in Moscow at the time. My soul path number is 7, derived by adding the month, day and year of my birth, and seven is a mystical number. For example, the number 7 is mentioned in the Bible 735 times, and it is found in the Book of Joshua where Joshua and the Israelites destroyed the walls of Jericho by walking around the city with the Ark of the Covenant for 7 days. It is found in the Book of Revelations where the 7th seal is opened, the 7th trumpet is heard and the 7th vial is opened.

Numerologists suggest the number 7 is an auspicious sign, denoting mysticism and psychic ability. But, other than so many number sevens in my birth, there was nothing else to suggest my supernatural gifts—except my astrological chart. Years later I was told my astrological chart contained the Yod of God or Finger of God which falls on Aquarius, Cancer and Aries. The Yod of God is a rare astrological aspect that involves any three planets or points in the horoscope that form a triangle, and mine falls on fire, water and air signs. The water sign of Cancer gives me a greater psychic ability and sensitivity, the air sign of Aquarius gives me the gift of prophecy, and the fire sign of Aries gives me the ability to speak my truth.

Shortly after my birth my great-grandmother, Katherine, returned from Israel, after traveling the world. She and her companion brought back a vial of water from the holy River Jordan, where Jesus was supposedly baptized by John the Baptist. The vial of water was used in my christening. Although it was a big deal then, now Jordan's holy water and the miracle water of Lourdes can be purchased on Amazon.com.

According to my parents I was a happy baby, always smiling and laughing, perhaps at my unseen friends. At age three, I acquired two invisible playmates I promptly nicknamed "Peek-a-Boo" and "Patoy." Although my invisible playmates slowly faded from my memory as I grew older, Mom said they seemed quite real to me, especially my descriptions of them and the conversations I enjoyed with them on a daily basis. I refused to divulge their messages. I believe they were my spirit guides. There are countless stories of children who see invisible friends or deceased relatives. As time goes by, usually around the age of seven or eight, children lose the ability to hear and see the Other Side.

Dr. Meg Blackburn Losey, in her book, *The Children of Now*, states a child loses his or her ability to see spirits because the child's parents discourage the child from having imaginary friends. Over time, a child forgets their ability to communicate with the Other Side, due to constant negative reinforcement. It is also suggested that when a child is born, he or she still remembers the "Other Side," residing in both worlds—the physical and spiritual the same time. There are also countless stories of small babies giggling as if someone tickled them or staring at the ceiling at an unseen presence.

Growing up was difficult for me because I felt like this wasn't my real home and I had been given the wrong body—a common trait for children who recall past lives. For many years I believed my parents had adopted me, but I can assure you I wasn't adopted, although adoption happened for my mother and was carried on.

Ghost Inside My Child debuted on My Lifetime Channel in 2014 and featured children who recalled past lives. Many of them under the age of five had terrifying dreams of a past life and couldn't sleep at night. One show was about a normal little girl from Australia began to have nightmares and crying spells. There was nothing physically wrong her, yet the nightmares persisted. As she grew older she began to cling to her mother, almost to the point of obsession. Finally, at the age of eight, she began to tell her mother about the nightmares that haunted her where she was standing on a roof top and a young girl is standing beside her and slips from the roof top to the ground. Hypnosis revealed that the sister that died from the fall was the girl's mother in a past life and she feared her best friend, her mother would die at a young age again and leave her. Further research uncovered that outlaws during the 1800s in Australia burned and looted ranch homes, often killing the people who lived there. The two girls heard the outlaws coming and went to the second story of the house to hide and that's when the sister fell to her death.

The new children are here to raise the planet's vibration—they vibrate at a much higher level. These children have increased psychic and telepathic gifts, past life recall, and possess genius abilities in the arts, music, math, and science. They also have innovative ideas for changing our world, and in some instances, have put their ideas to work. They are the old souls returning.

The first time I discovered I had spirit guides was at age seven (there's that mystical number again), when they saved me from certain death. One day, as I rode my bike home from first grade, I stopped at a grocery store to purchase a 'jawbreaker' candy. Popping the hard round candy into my mouth, I hopped back on my bike and started for home. Then it happened—I swallowed the jawbreaker, and it stuck in my throat, choking the life out of me! Seconds later I felt a hand slap me on the back, and the jawbreaker dislodged from my throat and fell to the street. When I turned around to thank my rescuer, I was shocked—no one was there.

That's when I realized unseen hands had saved my life, and

they have saved my life at seven times or more through the years. Hopefully, I haven't used up all my saves!

Again, at age seven, I experienced the paranormal while walking home from first grade, when a gigantic silver UFO hovered over me and seemed to follow me. Usually I arrived home in fifteen minutes, but on that day it took one hour, according to my frantic mother.

This encounter seemed to trigger nightly dreams of violent earth upheavals of volcanic eruptions, powerful earthquakes, tsunami waves, and hurricane-force winds. These dreams were so vivid, so real, that I knew I would, in my later years, witness earth disasters as my dreams had forewarned in 1957. Now we are seeing unprecedented weather, disastrous earthquakes, strange sink holes forming, unexplained booms heard worldwide, and increased volcanic eruptions. Clearly, something is happening to our planet, and I was forewarned of these events fifty-seven years ago.

Mostly I was a normal kid, who loved animals, riding horses, climbing trees, exploring caves, ice skating and swimming. The only difference between me and other children was my belief in spirits, telepathy, past lives and aliens, which my mother instilled in me from her paranormal beliefs and amazing psychic powers. I spent hours in school trying to levitate pencils with my mind. Several times I accomplished telekinesis, much to my surprise. From childhood into my teens, I felt ostracized because of my paranormal beliefs, and slowly I began to withdraw and remain quiet about my visions, sixth sense and dreams. In my teens I was branded a bit of an oddball, but thankfully, my mother was there to give me support on mystical things.

My paternal grandfather also noticed I was unusual, and nicknamed me "his little kooks." My grandfather and I had a special bond, perhaps because we were both Pisces, sensitive, and sometimes-misunderstood souls. Foss Manufacturing was known for the finest leather saddles throughout the Northwest. It was rumored my grandfather hid large sums of cash in the shop because of his distrust of banks after the Great Depression. If he had hidden money, it vanished soon after his death.

The last time I saw my grandfather he showed me his secret room in the shop, a loft room which he could retreat to for a little solitude. Several days later on December 7 (yes, 7 again) my father received a phone call from his brother in Contact, Nevada, informing him that Granddaddy had passed away from a massive heart attack, while walking up a hill. He had been inspecting his mining property that day. Only-eight-years-old, I was devastated by the news, and ran to my room sobbing that night, wishing I could communicate with him one more time. How I prayed that I could have one last conversation with Granddaddy, and tell him how much I loved and missed him. That's when I decided to write secret notes and hide them in the basement of his saddle shop. Those messages mysteriously vanished. Did an employee or my father discover the messages?—if they did, no one ever let on.

I believed Granddaddy heard my prayers and read my heartfelt messages because; several months later he paid me a visit.

Night after night, I heard strange noises throughout the house, and a metal cup in the bathroom falling to the floor. Then, one night, I woke with a start, sensing someone watching me. I opened my eyes to see a misty form of a man standing beside my bed. Scared out of my wits, I tried to call out to my parents, but I couldn't find my voice.

When people say they were paralyzed with fear, believe me... its true! It's not a metaphor, it's a fact. I couldn't move or call out. Finally, I grabbed the covers and dove under them until day break, praying the ghostly apparition was gone and, thankfully, it was.

Next morning I confided in Mom about my ghostly visitation, knowing she might explain what I witnessed. She suggested that it was Granddaddy's spirit, that he was probably aware of my grief from his passing and wanted to comfort me, per my request. "Mom, Granddaddy looked a lot like Dad does now. Why would he look so young and so much thinner?" Mother found the family photograph album and pulled out a photograph of Granddaddy as a young man in military uniform and said, "Is this your ghostly friend?" I instantly recognized my ghostly visitor as my grandfather. She then suggested that spirits of deceased people often appear much younger, a time when they looked and felt their best. If I had seen him as I had known him, I'm sure that I might have accepted his visitation.

Author's paternal grandfather as a young man as he appeared to her after his death

The ghostly noises continued throughout the house, but my grandfather never materialized again. No doubt he knew his visitation had frightened me, but the poltergeist activity continued, perhaps his way of letting me know he was there. Suddenly I had become clairaudient and given the ability to hear spirit voices. A male voice often called out my name early in the morning. I finally asked my grandfather or spirit guides to stop waking me, unless they had something important to say.

I wasn't the only one who sensed something paranormal in our house. Mom claimed she heard creepy sounds and loud banging whenever she was alone in the basement doing laundry. Whenever she heard heavy footsteps walking across the living room floor, she'd race up stairs and find nothing unusual. Our Labrador dog Lady also sensed something amiss in our house, barking constantly at an unseen presence.

Both my parents believed in the paranormal, but it was Mom who recalled a past life as a male Chinese laborer, forced to build the

Great Wall of China, and was buried inside the Great Wall. This was a little known fact until years later when archaeological excavations uncovered evidence of human remains inside The Great Wall.

Mom also possessed the ability to astral project, when people often witnessed her in two places at once. Realizing my psychic gift, Mom used a deck of regular playing cards to increase my psychic ability, by asking me to visualize the card's color or suit. My accuracy was phenomenal. I also had the ability to identify the caller on the phone before answering, and this was long before caller I.D., voice mail or answering machines. In fact, I also discovered that I could will a friend to call me at a certain time, which I stopped because I felt it was wrong to force my will on another person, even if it only involved a phone call.

My next near-death experience happened at age ten, after a large snow storm had dropped a foot of heavy, wet snow on Southern Idaho. We lived in the country, and a snowplow had pushed the snow into a tall snowbank on the side of the road. This was perfect for a snow cave. While my younger sister, Kathy, played in the house, I dug a large opening into the snow bank and crawled deep inside, until I was covered in snow. That's when the entire snow cave collapsed. I was buried by the heavy snow, unable to move or call out for help. I was buried and suffocating, realizing Mom wouldn't know where to find me under such deep snow. I was going to die. As I gasped for air, while still trying to escape from the snow, I prayed for an angel to save me from this death. Then a miracle happened—my body was lifted straight up through the crushing weight of snow. In the next minute, I stood on the side of the road beside the snow bank, freed from my snowy grave. I shook off the snow and rushed home, shouting at the top of my lungs, "Thank you!" to the unseen hand that saved my life again. Was the unseen hand my grandfather or my two little guardian angels/spirit guides I named Peek-a-Boo and Patoy at age three? Whoever watched over me must have felt I had much more to do in life.

At age fifteen my father purchased a 1952 faded-blue Studebaker for me from my Uncle Martin. I was thrilled to own my first car, even though it was the ugliest car I'd ever seen! My first driving adventure was with my sister Kathy, on a country road. Speeding, I drove toward a major intersection and applied the brakes and discovered the brakes were gone. I screamed, "Kathy, pray!" as we sailed through the busy intersection. It was a miracle as we coasted to a stop on the opposite side of the intersection. We sat in the car dazed; realizing we had just escaped what might have been a fatal car crash. Again, my spirit guides were there to make sure my sister and I made it across the busy street.

It was in December 1978 that I joined a friend and his co-worker on a flight from Portland, Oregon, to Wenatchee, in central Washington, in a single engine plane. Despite my ill-feeling not to go due to a large snowstorm predicted from northern Oregon to Washington, I went along. Only twenty minutes into the flight we hit extreme turbulence as ice began to form on the windshield; a dangerous sign for large or small planes. The charter pilot reassured us that we would be fine, yet all I could think about was the single engine plane that crashed from ice build-up carrying rock and roll stars Buddy Holly, The Big Bopper, and Ritchie Valens on January

23, 1959.

As we flew over Mount St. Helens and Wenatchee Mountains in a heavy snowstorm the ice continued to build-up on the plane. I prayed harder than I ever before, and it seemed my prayers were answered when the Wenatchee airport came into view, although covered in two feet of snow. We landed safely.

I've had more than my share of near death experiences—I've survived four near-fatal asthma attacks since my teen years, I nearly hemorrhaged to death from a non-malignant mass on my uterus requiring a blood transfusion and emergency surgery, and I was nearly strangled to death by an abusive boyfriend. Again, in 2006, my spirit guides were there to save my husband, a friend and me from a head-on car collision. My husband, our friend Lani and I decided to drive to Reno for a vacation, taking Highway 95 that loops through Oregon and down to the Nevada border. Spirit told me to drive, so I convinced my husband to let me drive first. As we passed the little town of Jordan Valley on the two lane highway in heavy traffic, I sensed something was going to happen. Several mobile homes went by headed north, and suddenly an older car turned into our lane, heading directly for us at 65 miles per hour. I calmly took my foot off the gas and turned the car into the shoulder, without going into the embankment. After the incident, my husband said the car missed us by inches as it continued down the highway in the wrong lane. If the car had been driven by a drunk, he didn't swerve but continued down the wrong side of the highway until the car was out of sight. I tried to contact local police on my cell phone but couldn't get any service, so we kept driving. As soon as we arrived in Reno, I contacted Jordan Valley's police department and asked if there had been any car accidents that day. None were reported. Was this a phantom car? The events of that day seemed surreal and dreamlike.

I can't explain what happened that day, I just know that my spirit guides were there to protect us from a horrible crash, and I'm eternally indebted for their love and guidance. No matter where I travel, I always say a prayer for divine protection and bring my *wotai* stone that I found in Yellowstone National Park, and I feel protected.

I have no doubt we are destined to live on earth to accomplish our lessons and mission. Recently I read the miracle story of a 6-year-old boy named Nathan Woessner from Chicago who was buried at Mount Baldy, under a huge sand dune that swallowed him in an eleven foot hole for four hours, He survived without any complications or brain damage. Paramedic Buddy Kasinger who treated Nathan in the lifeguard pickup truck said, "For God to bring this child back, it makes me wonder what's going to happen to Nathan's life and what kind of difference he's going to make."

Chapter Two
Saving Kathy

My sister Kathy was born three years after I entered the world. As children we had the normal sibling feuds, but as much as I loved and adored my baby sister, she could be an absolute pain in the butt! She constantly borrowed my clothes and returned them either dirty or torn, thus producing some lively arguments and hair pulling. One summer day I had a premonition about Kathy dying young. To appease the angry gods who wanted to take her life, I made her walk backwards for one full day to change her fate. Not only did I make her walk backwards that day, but she couldn't step on the cracks in the sidewalks.

Kathy, age 2 and Betsey, age 5

My poor sister must have thought I was getting even for the clothes she had ruined of mine, but nonetheless she obeyed my 'half-brain' instructions. Thankfully, Kathy did live many more years, but died at the age of fifty. Sadly, our relationship remained rocky, and for many years we didn't speak because of petty differences and misunderstandings. I was greatly upset by her refusal to talk during those years and how we had wasted precious years quarreling over insignificant things that didn't really matter.

By 1983, Kathy had divorced her first husband and moved to Los Angeles to be near Mom and me. That same year she met Hector, her future husband, at a disco club in the Studio City. Hector, originally from Argentina, was twenty-five years Kathy's senior, like my first husband Joe, and even stranger they had the same birthday, September 25. Kathy and Hector eventually married in Las Vegas after six months of dating, and moved into an apartment in Sherman Oaks, California. I realized that this was no accident, but lessons Kathy, Hector, Joe and I had planned long before we were born.

Soon Kathy discovered she was pregnant, and began experiencing severe pain and heavy bleeding. Although she had an adult son from her first marriage, she longed to have a baby with Hector. But something was wrong. Kathy's gynecologist determined she had an ectopic or tubal pregnancy, which happens when the fertilized egg stays in a woman's fallopian tube. In Kathy's case, the fertilized egg attached to one of her ovaries. Emergency surgery was required, her gynecologist urged. But Kathy and Hector didn't have health insurance and hospitals in Los Angeles wanted either full payment or insurance for admittance. Kathy couldn't stop crying, and I was frightened for her. "Don't cry, sis, I'll find a hospital for you," I tried to reassure her. At that moment I flashed on my childhood vision of Kathy dying young. I was determined fate wasn't going to take her…not now. That's when I prayed with all my heart for my spirit guides and angels to save her. I called every hospital listed in the Los Angeles Yellow Pages, pleading for help. Each hospital said they couldn't admit Kathy unless she had money or insurance. Finally, a Beverly Hills hospital referred me to Good Samaritan Hospital in East Los Angeles, a non-profit organization, willing to take Kathy without money. Hector drove Kathy to the Good Samaritan Hospital, where she was rushed into emergency surgery.

Thankfully, Kathy recovered without any complications; however, Kathy's surgeon said that if she had waited an hour longer they couldn't have saved her. After her near-death experience, I wondered if there's a destined plan we bring into this world or do we have the ability to change events in our life, through Creator's gift of free will? The answer I received from spirit is that even though we make a decision before our birth to die on a certain date, in a certain way, after we have accomplished our life mission; we create our destiny each and every day. There are no accidents in life, only spiritual lessons. We are spiritual beings first, and our true home is the spiritual realm, not our physical world. As spiritual beings, we decide to explore physical reality, and explore all human emotions: love, hate, jealousy, envy, compassion, and fear. This includes pain, both physical and mental. The Creator of All, God, Allah, Great Spirit, or whatever you prefer to call the loving force that created all that is, gave us free will to explore and evolve—what a magnificent miracle.

Chapter Three
A Guy Named Joe

In order for you to truly understand me and how my early life shaped me and my spiritual beliefs, I must digress and take you back to 1967, a time when my life drastically changed. I was given a vision of the next event in my life. It was autumn, one year after Kathy and I returned to Idaho after living in Hollywood, California with our great Aunt Grace. I began experiencing recurring dreams of palm trees and white sandy beaches. The dreams were so vivid I'd awaken and feel I was back in Los Angeles again.

Kathy and I were sent to live with our eccentric great aunt Grace earlier that year. Our parents felt that they could reconcile their marriage if we weren't there. Unfortunately, their plan failed miserably. After Kathy and I return to Idaho, their arguments and fights grew more violent, to the point I feared someone might be seriously injured or killed. My father had a nasty temper, especially after drinking, and Mom, instead of walking away, always fought back. Their relationship was a time bomb waiting to explode.

That time bomb exploded one late autumn evening; an argument so horrible it turned into a physical fight. Mom ran out of the house and jumped in the car to drive away. Before she could start the car, Dad hurled a wooden box through the driver's window. Glass shattered everywhere, giving Mom a deep gash on her forehead. She stumbled out of the car, dazed and bloody, as Dad grabbed the car keys. Mom struggled to get away, while I fought him off. I escaped Dad's grasp as the three of us, Mom, Kathy, and I, ran down the dirt road all the way to a neighbor's home in the Snake River Canyon, a mile from the Dierkes' Lake resort my parents had purchased six years earlier.

Two days later Mom and I secretly boarded a Greyhound bus for Los Angeles with only two suitcases and two hundred dollars we had borrowed from a friend. Kathy didn't want to leave; she decided to stay in Idaho to finish her high school education. Because Kathy and Dad got along well, I wasn't worried that he'd harm her. His anger always seemed directed at Mom and me. I reminded of Mom and how I stood up to him and that angered him. Many times I fought him off to protect Mom whenever their arguments became violent. Because Mom feared for her life as well as mine, she decided we had to get away as far from Idaho as possible or Dad would track us down and bring us back to Twin Falls, which had happened before.

When we arrived at the Greyhound Bus terminal in downtown Los Angeles, Charles, an African American in his mid-forties, was there to drive us to a temporary motel. Charles was chauffeur and butler for Mark Lindsay, lead singer for the rock and roll band, Paul Revere and the Raiders, as well as for music producer Terry Melcher, and his girlfriend, actress Candice Bergen, at their Beverly Hills home.

***

I met Charles a few months earlier while Kathy and I attended school in Los Angeles, living with our great Aunt Grace. One weekend I persuaded a school friend to drive to Mark Lindsay's hillside home at 10050 Cielo Drive, off Benedict Canyon, in Beverly Hills. As I tried to open the iron gate, Charles confronted me and asked why I wanted inside the private gated residence. He thought I was just another groupie until I explained that I met Mark and the Raiders three years earlier during their concert at my parents' lake resort in southern Idaho.

At the time Mark and Terry were travelling, so Charles offered a tour of the house's interior. I was thrilled at first. Although the house was spacious and nicely decorated, it felt creepy, dark, and foreboding to me. I quickly left the house, glad to be outside feeling something really foreboding there. I sensed a darkness there and felt something bad was going to happen although I couldn't imagine what it could be until three years later when the horrific news broke on August 9, 1969, that actress Sharon Tate, wife of director Roman Polanski, and four of her friends—coffee heiress Abigail Folger, hairdresser Jay Sebring, writer Wojciech Frykowski, and Steven Parent, were murdered by Charles Manson's followers, in the same Cielo Drive house I had toured in 1966. Sharon Tate was eight months pregnant at the time. Sharon's husband, director Roman Polanski, was in London wrapping up a movie and had planned to return home for the birth of his child. Polanski became famous for his 1968 supernatural thriller, *Rosemary's Baby,* starring Mia Farrow and John Cassavetes, based on the best-selling 1967 novel by Ira Levin. Here's the bizarre part of the Tate murders—in the story, *Rosemary's Baby,* supernatural events take place where people suddenly die around Farrow's character. She then becomes pregnant and is told by cult members that her baby is the spawn of Satan.

The murders were one of the most gruesome murders in L.A. history. The next day, Manson and his followers continued their bloody rampage, killing Leo and Rosemary LaBianca. A total of seven people were dead by Manson's cult followers. According to news reports, Terry Melcher had been introduced to ex-con and aspiring musician Charles Manson in 1968, after Beach Boy Dennis Wilson had picked up hitchhiking Manson. For a time, Melcher was interested in recording Manson's music. Manson auditioned for Melcher, but Melcher declined to sign him. Also, Wilson decided not to continue any further projects with Manson, including a documentary on the Manson family and their hippie commune existence. This angered Manson. Melcher, Candice Bergen and Mark Lindsay moved out of the Cielo Drive home not long after splitting from Manson, and the house was then leased to film director Roman Polanski and his wife, Sharon Tate.

Investigators theorized that Manson wanted revenge for Melcher's rejection. It was believed Manson thought Melcher still lived in the house, however it was later revealed by a Manson family member that Manson did know that Melcher no longer lived there.

Today I still get ice cold chills thinking I toured that house in 1966. Why did I experience such an ominous feeling in the house three years before the event? Was the house haunted then? Did I perceive the future or did I just feel an evil presence in the house? Even before the 1969 murders, the house had a spooky history, according to some authors. Years later, the original Tate hillside house was bulldozed and a large villa was built on the property. Some investigators claim they have seen Sharon Tate's ghost late at night. Perhaps something evil happened on that hillside in Laurel Canyon decades before and the residual negative energy had never dissipated.

Ghosts are considered "intelligent" because they interact with the living inhabitants of a house or building. In some cases, ghosts are held earthbound by a traumatic event and haunt the structure, unable to accept they have died. There are also memory hauntings, caused by extreme emotion— anger, stress, revenge, or fear. The emotion forces the person's energy out of its physical body so quickly that it leaves an imprint in the actual molecular structure of the location, and events are replayed like a movie.

***

Charles drove Mom and me to a small motel on the corner of La

Cienega Boulevard and Little Santa Monica Boulevard, where we stayed for two weeks while searching the L.A. Times classified section for jobs. We survived on avocado sandwiches to conserve our finances. After two weeks Mom and I were hired at Union Bank in downtown Los Angeles, despite our lack of banking experience. Within two more weeks we moved into a tiny apartment on Sixth Street, a block from Wilshire Boulevard.

The day we moved into our new abode, I noticed a handsome man lying on a lounge chair, sunbathing beside the small apartment swimming pool. My first impression was that he looked uncannily like Cuban actor/comedian Desi Arnaz, Lucille Ball's husband, with his dark blue eyes, black, wavy hair, and deep tan. He introduced himself as Joe. Days later I mentioned his remarkable resemblance to Desi Arnaz, and he bragged that he and Desi were distant cousins, and met for lunch at the Desilu Studios on Little Santa Monica Boulevard. Desi was still filming a later version of the *I Love Lucy Show*, renamed *The Lucille Ball-Desi Arnaz Show*.

Joe had an amazing gift for story-telling and great sense of humor, a personality trait I was drawn to from the beginning. Joe's favorite story was how he escorted the famous singing duo, Sonny and Cher out of Ben Frank, a famous Hollywood restaurant on Sunset Boulevard. As restaurant manager he felt bad about the incident, but the restaurant policy stated patrons without shoes could not be served, and Sonny and Cher were barefoot hippies. They left the restaurant without creating a scene.

Romance never entered my mind until months later.

Lucille Ball and Desi Arnaz

L to R. Joe on our wedding day and his best man John

Thanksgiving arrived and Joe, Mom, and I were invited to dinner at a mutual friend's home for dinner. After dinner, Joe kissed me goodnight, and sparks flew. This was the beginning our winter-spring relationship. Years later, after my sister Kathy married Hector, I made more discoveries about Joe and Hector: they were born on the identical day and month, September 25, Joe was twenty-five years my senior like Hector was twenty-five years Kathy's senior, both were raised Catholic, and both were Latin, Hector from Argentina, and Joe's parents from Cuba. This was beyond coincidence—we had past lives together. Being involved with a man old enough to be my father, who had fathered three children, now adults, from his first marriage, and who was currently paying child support for his fourth child from his second marriage on a meager chef's salary, sounded like disaster. Yet, somehow I knew Joe and I were fated to be together for lessons unlearned in past lives.

Joe was born in Tampa, Florida, and raised in New York by his American-Cuban mother, Mary. Joe's Cuban father, Jack, abandoned the family when Joe was a young boy living in New York, leaving his mom to care for five children. Joe later served in World War II and the Korean War. It was during the Korean War that Joe was severely injured by shrapnel and returned to his Wisconsin home to recover. He claimed car accidents and fist fights had broken almost every bone in his body.

June 4, 1968, arrived and I woke from a peculiar dream that haunted me for days. In the dream, a gypsy held my hand, and with her long red nails cut a cross in the middle of my palm. My hand dripped with blood. Long ago I had learned that if my dream appeared life-like, it was a warning of a future event, but sometimes the symbolism wasn't clear until after the event had taken place. The message seemed clear—the gypsy cutting my lifeline meant a life would be cut short, and the cross and blood meant someone important would die in a martyred way. I sensed the cross also meant someone Catholic.

The next day, June 5, Senator Robert Kennedy, who had

scored a major victory in winning the California primary, was scheduled to speak that evening at the Ambassador Hotel on Wilshire Boulevard, only four blocks from where Mom and I lived on Sixth Street. Shortly after midnight, we woke to sirens screaming and emergency red lights flashing everywhere from police cars and ambulances. We switched on the radio to hear news reports that Senator Kennedy had been shot and seriously injured. The news reports claimed that a few minutes after midnight, Kennedy left the ballroom after his speech and walked through the hotel kitchen after being told it was a shortcut, despite being advised to avoid it by his bodyguard, FBI agent Bill Barry.

Sirhan Sirhan, a 24-year-old Palestinian, had waited with the crowd in the kitchen passageway and opened fire with a 22-caliber revolver, hitting Kennedy three times, and injuring five other people. George Plimpton, former decathlete Rafer Johnson, and former professional football player Rosey Grier wrestled Sirhan Sirhan to the ground. Kennedy was transported to Good Samaritan Hospital where he died the next day, June 6, 1968.

I'd be remiss if I didn't include a conversation I had in 1974, while working at CBS News in Hollywood. A female newscaster confided that she was at the Ambassador Hotel that night, standing in the kitchen near Robert Kennedy when he was shot. She watched another man shoot Robert Kennedy from behind and disappear in the crowd while confused on-lookers and several people wrestled Sirhan Sirhan to the floor.

I was stunned by her revelation and asked why she didn't go to the authorities about the other man she witnessed there. She replied without hesitation, "Are you kidding? Do you know how many people mysteriously died after JFK's assassination in Dallas? I don't have a death wish!"

I prayed for Robert Kennedy's soul for days, wondering why I had been shown a symbolic dream of his death. Was my dream part of a destined event, or was it possible to change time lines and what appeared to be a destined event? I have always believed the past, present and future exist simultaneously, as theorized by quantum physicists.

What if President John Kennedy had heeded his secretary's warning to cancel his trip to Dallas? Perhaps there is a parallel world where JFK didn't go to Dallas.

The answer that spirit provided was that both Robert and John Kennedy had chosen their untimely deaths, and nothing could have prevented the prime events from happening. Their deaths were lessons that would one day be unveiled. I do know their deaths involved family secrets and something involving their father, Joseph P. Kennedy.

My next precognitive dreams from my spirit guides began Saturday, February 6, 1971. Each morning for days, I recalled a vivid dream where Mom, Joe and I survived a powerful L.A. earthquake. When I mentioned my dream to Mom and Joe, telling them how I sensed a powerful earthquake soon, Mom trusted my intuition, but Joe joked about it and didn't buy my sixth sense warning.

Tuesday arrived and I woke earlier than usual, at 5:00 a.m., dressed for my new job at Stern, Meyer and Fox brokerage firm in

Beverly Hills, and started to head out the door to catch the bus on Wilshire Boulevard. At exactly 6:00 a.m. a loud moan grew into a roar until the entire apartment swayed violently for what seemed minutes. I was knocked to the floor and tried crawling to the doorway to open the door and escape, but couldn't. The door wouldn't budge. Twelve seconds later, the earth stopped shaking, but I continued to shake, scared out of my wits. This was my first big earthquake and I felt completely helpless.

Just as my dream had shown me, Mom, Joe, and our friends were unharmed during the big earthquake. While buildings along Wilshire Boulevard sustained broken windows, the worst damage was in the San Fernando Valley. Overpasses collapsed, buildings collapsed, and a section of the Northridge Veteran's Hospital collapsed. An estimated 65 lives were lost on February 9 from the 6.6 magnitude earthquake.

Again I was forewarned by my loving spirit guides.

A few months later, Joe accepted a well-paying chef's job at Rococo's restaurant in Woodland Hills, where he now lived. I moved in with him. He worked long hours, and complained of lethargy and nightly fever, accompanied by a persistent cough. I was concerned about his health and urged him to see a doctor, but he insisted it was nothing more than smoker's cough.

Then, one day, Joe looking as if he'd seen a ghost, said, "I smell lilacs, my aunt's favorite perfume. I think she's here to say I'm going to die soon." Joe was adamant about his aunt's presence, so I tried to make light of his fear of death by teasing him that it was his over-active imagination. I sensed, like Joe, that his aunt's visit was to prepare him for the Other Side. Our deceased loved ones often prepare us for our journey to the Other Side. Sometimes their visit can be to comfort us in our time of sorrow and pain, and to let us know they still watch over us and guide us along our earthly journey. Validations from our loved ones can be subtle, like their favorite perfume permeating the air, a vivid dream, or hearing their favorite song played whenever you turn on the radio.

Joe was admitted to Kaiser Hospital, on Sunset Boulevard, for observation. Test after test returned normal, yet he continued to lose weight and feel lethargic. Finally, fluid was discovered on his right lung and drained. He was released from the hospital, but he still felt lethargic. Nothing else was found to explain his continuing illness, as Joe's doctors remained baffled.

April arrived, and Mom joined a Beverly Hills dating service. Her first phone call was from a man who identified himself only as Maurice. On their first date, Maurice picked Mom up in front of the Beverly Hills agency in his powder-blue Cadillac. Mom later described Maurice as a large-framed man with sagging jowls, reminiscent of a sad hound dog. But it was his poker face and reticent manner that baffled her the most as they drove to Newport Beach for dinner.

Out of the blue, he said, "Are you afraid of me?"

"Why should I be, Maurice?" Mom shot back.

"For God's sake, call me Moe," he bellowed.

During dinner Moe was quiet, and it wasn't until he drove Mom home that he tossed a hardback book into her lap and ordered, in an unexpectedly booming voice, "Read it, my brother wrote it."

Moe stood beside the car waiting for Mom's reaction, while she took her time and studied the novel's cover. The book cover read, *The Exorcist* by William Peter Blatty. She then flipped open the dust jacket and read the blurb. The book was about the demonic possession of a twelve-year-old girl named Regan MacNeil, daughter of a famous actress, and the Jesuit psychiatrist priest who attempted to exorcise the demon from her. Before Mom could finish the next paragraph, Moe grabbed the book back, resting it on the roof of the car, and scrawled his brother's name, William Peter Blatty, on the flyleaf, explaining that his youngest brother had given him power of attorney to autograph copies of his novel. Mom had heard of *The Exorcist,* but didn't realize it was just beginning to receive literary acclaim.

This was the beginning of Mom's stormy relationship with Moe Blatty. Several months later they wed at a Las Vegas chapel with a minister that did an Elvis impression. This was Moe's first marriage. Mom soon realized that much of Moe's bizarre behavior and off-the wall humor was from his insecurity. Their honeymoon was spent at Bill's vacation home in Aspen, Colorado, overlooking the famous ski resort. Two days later, Bill arrived, to work on *The Exorcist* screenplay. She and Moe saw little of Bill during their visit.

Afterwards, Mom had the time of her life, travelling with Moe to New York City, to visit Moe's sister. They also dined at fine restaurants, including The Palm Restaurant in West Los Angeles, one of Bill Blatty's investments since the huge literary success. Meanwhile I was about to enter the darkest time of my life, which would test my faith and spiritual beliefs.

L to R: William "Bill" Peter Blatty, Betsey's Mom Bette, and Maurice "Moe" Blatty,

Chapter Four
The Signs are Everywhere

One year later Joe and I shared our wedding vows at the Las Vegas Courthouse, accompanied by our two best friends, John and Peggy. I continued to feel marrying Joe was a huge mistake, but I continued to ignore the still, small voice within. After the wedding, Joe and I drove through Nevada, headed for a new life in Southern Idaho. Joe was tired of Los Angeles life, and was anxious to move back to Twin Falls, Idaho, my childhood home.

We drove through the night on Nevada's desolate Highway 93, and as midnight neared, I noticed hundreds of meteors falling from the sky, like Fourth of July fireworks. I had never seen such an incredible meteor shower. Suddenly, an enormous green fireball streaked toward us. I screamed, Joe slammed on the brakes, as the meteor exploded somewhere over the vast Nevada desert. Joe pulled the car to the side of the highway, where we sat quietly for what seemed minutes, unable to speak. All the while, I wondered if the meteor was a harbinger of tough times ahead. My intuition proved right!

Betsey and Joe on their wedding day

By now Joe had lost several more pounds. He had looked and felt sickly on our wedding day, and I sensed time was running out for him. Although his doctors had given him a clean bill of health, I suspected he was seriously ill. In Twin Falls we rented a two-bedroom duplex across the street from my father's house. Each day, Joe became weaker until I finally took matters into my own hands and made an appointment for him to see a local doctor, recommended by a neighbor.

Joe was given a brief physical, and was declared perfectly

healthy by the small town doctor. The doctor notified Social Security that Joe could return to work, which stopped his disability checks. I was furious that this doctor gave Joe a clean bill of health, when it was obvious Joe was sick. And to make matters worse, Joe's ten-year-old daughter from Los Angeles was sent to live with us because his ex-wife couldn't handle her. I wasn't ready to be a stepmother while dealing with Joe's declining health. It was all too much to handle.

Joe was too weak to work, so I took a secretarial job at a local brokerage firm to help cover food and rent, but it wasn't enough to cover other bills and living expenses. Soon we were forced to apply for food stamps, which was both embarrassing and demoralizing. Dad surprised us by his compassion and gave us money and food, but it was still hard making ends meet. Suddenly I was seeing another side to my father, a side he never expressed to me as a child.

Through the years he had belittled me any way he could—I was never smart enough. I am dyslexic and was never diagnosed with it during the late 1950s, and this caused me great difficulty in reading and in math. One night my father lost his patience with me trying to get me to understand multiplication, and whipped me with a horse whip he had made. The whip stung my legs and angry red welts appeared. I prayed silently for help. Even Mom tried to reason with him, but to no avail.

As I cried something strange happened—my prayer was answered. A house in the neighborhood caught fire and people were rushing from their homes to find out what had happened, which caused Dad to stop his punishment. This was the father I remembered as a child, a man with little patience who seldom gave compliments or expressed his love. His drinking always brought out the worst in him for both my mother and me. Now I was seeing a different father who hugged me, and even said he loved me.

After Mom and I left Idaho for Los Angeles he had disowned me, and it took many years for him to contact me again. Now I wanted to know my father, despite the wall he'd put up. I wondered if his father or mother had been abusive to him which had started the abusive pattern. On occasions when he was alone I tried to have candid discussions about the past, but he always changed the subject or blamed Mom for their divorce. Never once did he admit that alcohol might have contributed to their dysfunctional marriage.

By early December, Joe was admitted to the Veteran's Hospital in Boise, Idaho, a two-hour drive from Twin Falls. Tests were again conducted, including a biopsy of a lump under his arm. The biopsy revealed the unthinkable—Joe had advanced Hodgkin's disease, a lymphatic cancer. After several weeks of chemotherapy, Joe began to improve and put on weight again, giving us hope for his cancer remission. By the time April arrived Joe finally received his disability Social Security checks, which included six months of withheld checks. Thanks to Idaho's Senator Frank Church's investigation into Joe's case, and the subsequent waiver of the obligatory board review, he received his disability checks.

Meanwhile Joe's daughter flew back to her mother in L.A. Joe had decided he wanted to return to Hialeah, Florida, to be near his elderly mother, Mary, and other relatives he hadn't seen in years.

Dad thought Joe was making a huge mistake leaving Idaho where he had received excellent care from Idaho's Tumor Institute in Boise, but Joe wasn't going to be deterred from his decision.

The move proved to be a mistake as Dad predicted. Joe spent hours in and out of the Veteran's Hospital in Hialeah, where a few doctors but mostly interns drew blood from his sore arms, and pumped more chemotherapy into his weakened body. Each time he returned home to our Hialeah apartment, he experienced severe chills, fever and vomiting. One day, Joe called me into the bedroom, his head propped up against several pillows. Soaked in perspiration with his lips blue and trembling, he said reverting to his Bronx slang, "I have an *idear*. I want you to leave me. It's not fair you have to care for a man old enough to be your father."

How could Joe suggest such a thing? I thought. "I love you and I'm not leaving," I said, tears streaming down my face. I reminded him that we said a vow, till death do us part. We held each other, and cried.

Life had already taught me that there are no accidents in life, only lessons, and that Joe and I had been brought together to work out lessons of love, patience, and forgiveness, unlearned during past incarnations. Neither fate nor karma had thrust me into this situation. On the contrary, I believed Joe and I were together because we loved each other. This was my soul's experience of unconditional love, compassion, and service for a soul I had known in past lives.

But my depression and frustration grew each day, as I watched Joe's personality change. Doctors had prescribed Percodan, a codeine-related pain medication, as well as several other prescriptions that had adverse side effects that made him irritable. The least little thing sent him into a verbal tirade. Several of Joe's outbursts were directed at his mother and that sent her into tears. I tried to explain to Mary that it was the medicine affecting Joe and not her, but she didn't understand. Mary was deeply hurt, and believed her son no longer loved her.

Months passed, and Joe and I wanted out of Florida's humidity, and away from his less than friendly relatives. After years of absence from his family, Joe discovered he had grown away from them. Most of his family spoke only Spanish, or little English, and to make matters worse, Joe had forgotten most of the Spanish he learned as a child. I rarely went out with friends until one evening I jumped at the opportunity to join a co-worker for a meditation with a well-known medium at his home in Coral Gables, an exclusive area of Miami. Joe's close friend, Walter, offered to take care of Joe while I was out.

Although I'm psychic, sometimes it's hard to see the future when your life is in complete turmoil and you are dealing with someone's illness or terminal cancer, like I was dealing with Joe. I needed some spiritual guidance. Inside the spacious home, ten people were seated at a large table in the dining room. I was introduced to the group, including Edward, the medium, effeminate man with silver hair and light blue eyes. I sat down beside him and immediately he singled me out. "We have a new visitor tonight, I see." He paused as if listening to voices and continued, "Tonight my spirit guides tell me that you have an olive-green sweater tucked away in your closet. Why don't you wear it?"

I gave him a quizzical look and said, "Sorry, but I don't."

"But you do! When you get home tonight, check your closet. My guides also want me to tell you that you have writing, psychic and medium abilities."

"Oh really?" I said, believing he was guessing and not really perceiving anything. He continued, "They say you'll write many books later in life, about paranormal subjects. You'll see, my dear."

I couldn't imagine writing would be in my future, not at the moment.

As the night progressed, Edward discussed our relationship to God, how we are part of God-energy, and capable of anything. He emphasized that we create our reality ever moment we take a breath. Nothing is impossible, he said. By the end of the evening my head was spinning with new concepts about the nature of reality. As I headed to the door and said goodbye to the group, Edward pulled me aside and said, "Be prepared, someone in your family will pass next year." I was stunned to hear this from Edward even though my dreams and intuition warned of Joe's death. I was still in denial.

As soon as I returned home, I went through my closet and found the olive-green sweater Edward had mentioned. He was right; I didn't like the sweater and never wore it!

The first death in the family had been my paternal grandfather and the second was my paternal grandmother. I was twelve-years-old when Grandmother died. I remember viewing her lifeless body in the coffin, and now I didn't want to think of Joe this way. At twenty-three, I was trying to maintain a brave front for Joe. Inwardly, I was terrified of losing my best friend and spouse.

Meanwhile, Mom left Moe after a big argument, and moved to Miami to be near us, accepting a job as a concierge at the luxurious Fontainebleu Hotel on Miami Beach. She couldn't stand Moe's continual ravings, "We're doomed!" or "Disaster, disaster!" whenever they drove through any of Los Angeles' canyons, or his fear of getting lost on the L.A. freeway system and running out of gas.

To ensure that Moe never ran out of gas, he'd pull into a service station, get out of the car, and stand beside the attendant; then wait for him to lift the gas nozzle after the tank was full. Then he'd seize the attendant's hand, like an eagle on its prey, and order him to top off the tank. Mom was totally embarrassed by his eccentric behavior. But the final straw was Moe's gambling habit, when he would disappear into the night for hours, returning the next morning. To decipher Moe's eccentricity, I read Bill Blatty's autobiography, *I'll Tell Them I Remember You*. In the book, Bill wrote about his parents, Mary and Peter, who arrived in America from Lebanon on a cattle boat, in 1921. Moe was one of five children born to Mary and Peter Blatty. According to Bill's autobiography, their father, Peter, abandoned the family when Bill was six-years-old. With no marketable skills, except selling her homemade quince jelly, Mary Blatty moved the children constantly to avoid bill collectors.

Moe and his four siblings all seemed to have phobias in varying degrees, but Moe's phobias and idiosyncrasies were probably the worst, due to his fear of heights, which manifested in some rather hilarious stories. One night at the Palm Restaurant in

West Los Angeles, now co-owned by Bill Blatty, Moe talked about his World War II experiences. He told us that he volunteered for the Army Air Corp the day after Pearl Harbor was bombed by the Japanese on December 7, 1941. He continued, "It was July 23 I was assigned to a newly formed B-17 crew as radioman-gunner. I decided to leap from the plane and parachuted down to the field."

We all chimed in, "Why did you jump out of the plane, Moe?"

"I didn't like the way the god-damned pilot flew the plane. He made me nervous," he said with a straight face.

We all laughed, while Moe maintained his dead-pan expression. He went on to tell us how his plane once came back from a strike at Ploesti with 153 flak holes in the side and an engine shot out. Maurice and his crew were heavily decorated for their gallantry on that mission.

While I listened to Moe's stories I couldn't help but think that Joe and Moe had known each other in a past life because of all their uncanny similarities: Joe's mother's name was Mary, like Moe's mother; both were the product of broken homes where their fathers abandoned the family; they were raised Catholic, they grew up in New York City as their mothers struggled to support them; and both men had four siblings. Even their names rhymed!

Throughout our lives we are drawn to people who have joined us in prior incarnations. So many times people find an instant attraction to someone because their subconscious recalls a past lifetime with that person. If certain lessons were not understood in those lifetimes, the same patterns and dramas will play out again and again, until lessons are learned. It's what I call the "cosmic boomerang."

Moe flew to Miami, and convinced Mom to return to Los Angeles with him, and before leaving, Moe and Mom invited Joe and me to dinner at a Tony's Lobster restaurant on Miami Beach. Having no fashion sense, Moe arrived in an orange-striped shirt that barely covered his protruding stomach, and wearing blue polyester pants. All the while we ate, Moe fidgeted at the restaurant, complaining through the entire dinner about the lousy service. In between the complaints he mumbled, "We're doomed! We're doomed!"

Joe lightened the mood by telling stories of the pranks he and his best friend, John, had pulled on their gullible friend, Eugene. Moe begrudgingly cracked a smile.

Betsey and her mother Bette at Tony's Restaurant

Privately, Moe confided to Mom that he was shocked by Joe's gaunt appearance, and suggested Joe return to Los Angeles to get better medical care. Shortly after Mom and Moe returned to Los

Angeles, Joe developed painful herpes zoster, also known as shingles. Huge puss-filled blisters covered his abdomen and back, accompanied by extreme pain and burning. The blisters took over a month to heal, but the pain persisted.

When Moe heard about Joe's shingles and continuing downturn, he suggested to Mom that we should return to Los Angeles, where Joe could get better medical care with the Veteran's Hospital in Northridge. Moe then offered to let us stay at their Wilshire condominium, until we could get our own place. Once again, Joe and I packed our belongings and drove across country, from Hialeah to Los Angeles, driving during the day and stopping at motels at night. We arrived in Los Angeles five days later, hopeful for better medical care.

A few months later Mom and Moe attended Bill's wedding to tennis pro Linda Tuero, his third marriage, at the Flamingo Hotel in Las Vegas. Mom sat next to Mario Puzo, one of her favorite authors, best known for his New York best-selling novel, *The Godfather,* and received an autographed napkin.

L to R: Bill Blatty's daughters, Moe, and author's mother, Bette, attending Bill's wedding to Linda at the Las Vegas Flamingo Hotel

Chapter Five
Spirit Steps In

Since the release of the New York best-selling novel, *The Exorcist,* William Peter Blatty had become a household name, with appearances on television and radio, and countless interviews in magazines and newspapers. *The Exorcist* remained on the New York Times bestseller list for 57 straight weeks, and was at the number one spot for 17 weeks. Book sales hit over 13 million copies in the United States alone. Reviews described the book as powerful, raw, profane, shocking, blood-chilling, and perhaps the most terrifying novel ever written.

After writing the screenplay, Bill was wrapping up the

filming of the movie in Georgetown with director William Friedkin. The movie was set to be released on Boxing Day, December 26, 1973.

Bill generously gifted his living siblings, Moe, Eddie, and his sister Alyce with a sizable amount of money. Moe proceeded to spend the money on risky investments while gambling in Gardena, even though he promised Bill he'd quit. Most nights, Moe gambled through the night, returning home early the next morning in a cantankerous mood because of his losses. Joe and I could see that Moe was less than thrilled to have us staying in his condominium after three weeks. One night, Joe and Moe had a heated argument which resulted in Moe pushing Joe around. Angered by Moe's outburst, we packed our belongings and drove to the valley to stay with Joe's friend, John, and his wife Peggy.

One month later we moved into a five-unit, two-bedroom apartment in Studio City. Joe continued his painful chemotherapy treatments at the Veteran's Hospital in Northridge, and every night I prayed for Joe's life to be spared. My nightmares of Joe's death continued, despite our return to Los Angeles, and how much we tried to stay optimistic. Spirit kept telling me to prepare for his death.

Mom's co-worker, Vera, mentioned that a meeting was scheduled about the controversial cancer drug, Laetrile, which had been banned by the FDA in the United States, but was available in Mexico and several other countries. Laetrile was a substance found naturally in the pits of apricots and other fruits. In articles about Laetrile, there were stories of people who experienced complete remissions from their cancers. But Laetrile treatments were expensive at the Tijuana Clinic, where Dr. Ernesto Contreras, a former Mexican Army pathologist, received from 100 to 200 new patients per month.

It was reported in 1980 that Steve McQueen went to Mexico for the Laetrile treatments as a last effort to cure his cancer. He died several months later on November 7, 1980.

After the meeting at the Ambassador Hotel, Moe declared Joe had to get the Laetrile treatments, no matter what the cost. He planned to ask Bill to finance the trip to Mexico, but he wanted to wait until *The Exorcist* movie had premiered after Christmas. This gave us renewed hope that Laetrile was Joe's miracle cure, but fate had other plans.

By Christmas, Moe phoned with exciting news—Bill wanted to meet us at his Malibu home in late January to discuss Joe's Laetrile treatments.

The Exorcist Movie Premiers

The Exorcist movie was released on Boxing Day, December

26, 1973, in all major cities. Everywhere it was shown, people stood in line for hours to get into theaters across the country. The movie grossed a staggering $66.3 million in one month. Reviewers called The Exorcist the most successful movie in cinema history.

L to R: Director William Friedkin and William Peter Blatty filming The Exorcist at Georgetown

I read the novel, and was shocked by Bill's use of profanity and the explicit description of a twelve-year-old girl possessed by demonic forces. I wondered if the movie would include such graphic scenes, and if it did, I really didn't care to see it. However, Moe let us know Bill insisted we see the movie before our meeting, so I agreed, for Joe's sake.

Mom, Moe, Joe, and I watched *The Exorcist* movie at a theater in Beverly Hills where people stood in lines that wrapped around two blocks. Moe told the theater manager his relationship to Bill, and immediately we were ushered to the front of the line. The special effects were remarkable, and the theme music of Tubular Bells was haunting, but several scenes were ridiculous like the scene where actress Linda Blair who played Regan, the possessed child, growled, spun her head 360 degrees, and vomited what looked like green-pea soup. Although I was appalled by the way Bill's novel and movie had portrayed Regan as a helpless victim, abused by demonic forces, I realized *The Exorcist* would make millions of people aware of the dark forces that reside in our world.

Oddly, Bill Blatty was best known in Hollywood for his comedy screenplays—movie hits like *A Shot in the Dark,* starring Peter Sellers; *What Did you Do in the War Daddy?; Darling Lilli; The Great Train Robbery* and *Promise Her Anything*. Bill claimed he had written *The Exorcist* to prove to studio executives that he could write more than comedy screenplays.

Bill's inspiration for *The Exorcist* came to him from an article that first appeared in the Washington Post in 1947, about the exorcism of a fourteen-year-old boy, named Roland Doe, from Mount Rainer, Maryland. Although there were strange events with the Roland Doe possession, it was nothing like Bill had written in his novel. Several books on Roland's case suggested he tried to contact his deceased aunt via the Ouija board, and, shortly afterwards, furniture began to move, a vase levitated, and a container of holy water smashed to the floor. The media hype for the movie included rumors of hauntings, and a jinxed movie set during the filming. There were double images that appeared on shots of Linda Blair. The most widely reported event was the death of Jack MacGown, who died two weeks after completing scenes as Burke Dennings, the director in the movie, who dies mysteriously. There were other deaths attributed to the movie, including Max Von Sydow's brother and Linda Blair's grandfather. However, most articles insisted it was all promotional hype by the studio.

For Bill the supernatural was real. He stated in his biography, *I'll Tell Them I Remember You,* that he believed there was life after death, especially after his mother's death. He believed that she had made her presence known to him by causing phones to fly through the air on their own accord on several occasions. He also had tried to contact the Other Side by experimenting with reel-to-reel tape recordings where unearthly voices or EVP (electronic voice phenomenon) spoke to him. He started with a blank reel of unused tape, set the tape recorder on slow and asked the question, *Does God exist?* Then he set the microphone to the highest setting, pushed the record button and waited three minutes. After the tape was replayed, a distinct male voice clearly spoke the word, *Lacey.* The second time he replayed the tape at a higher speed he heard the words, "Hope it," words he believed referred to his original question. Some of the experiments produced phrases like, *I know what you are thinking,* and *There's no space here,* and *Make them pray, Bill.*

Bill mailed a copy of the original tape to a friend at Columbia University, who ran it through a spectrograph. The analysis revealed that the voice couldn't be human. In order to have created such an effect, an artificial larynx would have had to have been built and programmed to say those words. There was no logical explanation as to how the word *Lacey* transformed into *Hope it* when played at high speed. Moe, a confirmed skeptic of the paranormal, remarked to

Mom that he listened to Bill's unearthly recordings and couldn't understand a "damned thing."

The morning after we saw the movie, Moe and Mom picked up Joe and me at our Studio City apartment, and drove us to Bill's Malibu home, off the Pacific Coast Highway. All the while, I was deep in thought, wondering what to expect from Bill Blatty. White sailboats scudded across the Pacific Ocean on this beautiful January day. While Moe parked his powder-blue Cadillac in Bill's circular driveway, Bill's wife Linda greeted us at the door and ushered us into the spacious beach home. Linda, a tennis professional, had originally met Bill, a tennis enthusiast, while he filming *The Exorcist* in Georgetown.

We sat in the kitchen looking at Linda's wedding album when Bill finally appeared from upstairs and shook Joe's hand and then mine. Bill wore white tennis shorts and white shirt, which contrasted with his swarthy skin and jet-black hair, but it was his light-blue eyes that caught me off guard. Joe and I were visibly nervous as Mom joked about *The Exorcist* and its frightening scenes while Moe only grumbled to himself. Bill finally motioned for Moe to follow him outside onto the deck, where they conversed for several minutes, and then they stepped back into the living room. Before Bill excused himself to continue writing, I asked him if he had seen any UFOs off the coast of Malibu after noting a telescope on his deck. He said he had seen some strange lights off the coast mentioned and then he excused himself to continue writing upstairs. Moe suddenly leapt from the sofa and headed to the foyer, stating it was time to leave. Before leaving, Bill came down from his upstairs office and said goodbye, shaking our hands again.

Back in the car Moe was quiet, and we were fearful to ask him if Bill would help Joe with the Laetrile treatments, but halfway home Moe finally opened up. "Bill is going to help Joe, but there's one condition—I drive him to the clinic in Mexico," he stated.

We all rolled our eyes as if to say, "Oh no, not Moe!"

Spirit Steps in Again

The following Wednesday Moe and Joe drove across the U.S. border to the clinic, outside Tijuana. Over the next few days, Joe underwent a battery of tests, and began his Laetrile treatments. Each night, they returned to their motel in San Ysidro, on the U.S. side of the border, a few miles south of San Diego. Each evening after work I phoned Joe and heard how Moe was driving him crazy with his complaints about the lousy restaurants and "God-awful" motel. Joe was anxious to get back to L.A. and away from Moe's complaints and ravings of, "We're doomed," and "Disaster, disaster."

It was after work on Friday that I quickly packed a small suitcase, gathered up our miniature poodle, Banacek, and took the 405 Freeway. I had to see Joe. On the long drive, my thoughts were on him. Two hours into the drive, without warning, cars ahead of me began to swerve and brake. The ten cars in front seemed to be moving in slow motion, spinning and swerving. Incredibly, not one car collided, but, as I slammed on my brakes, my car began a tailspin into oncoming traffic – at least, that's what I thought. But the next moment, I was alone on the freeway—not one car in sight! I quickly swung the car around and headed toward San Diego again, overwhelmed by the miracle that had taken place moments before.

Thinking back on all my near death experiences, I couldn't deny my invisible friends had once again saved my life.

When I arrived at the motel I found Moe pacing like an angry parent. "Where the hell have you been?" he scolded. I tried to explain my near accident on the freeway, but Moe wasn't interested in my story. Instead, he mumbled about the lousy hotel accommodations and said goodnight, retiring to his room. Joe was thrilled to see me and our dog. He described the clinic and the wonderful people he'd met through the week, some from Europe and Australia. We talked for a few more minutes and retired for the night, exhausted. While Joe slept, I noticed how his once thick, black hair had thinned, and his dark blue eyes were now shadowed and sunken. This wasn't the handsome man I had met when Mom and I first moved to Los Angeles.

The next morning Moe drove us through Tijuana to the modern stucco building, Del Mar Medical Center and Hospital, which overlooked the Pacific Ocean. People at the clinic were friendly, and anxious to tell their stories of hope. They came from the United States, Europe, Australia and Canada. Their stories of courage and faith touched us and gave us renewed hope. After Joe received his dosage of medication, we returned to San Ysidro for dinner.

Sunday morning I drove back to Los Angeles, leaving Moe and Joe behind to buy two month's supply of Laetrile before their return home on Monday. Moe concealed the medication in the trunk of his Cadillac so they could get past U.S. Customs without having the medicine confiscated.

Each day Joe took the Laetrile but his weight continued to drop from his already gaunt frame. He refused to return to the V.A. Hospital in Northridge, even though his condition had worsened. He insisted he could beat the cancer, and began jotting notes for a memoir. He called me into the bedroom one day, and handed me his notes. At the top of the paper he had written his friend's name, Louis L'Amour, known for his best-selling Western novels. Joe had met Louis when he first arrived in Hollywood. I read on: *Children calling me Joe instead of Daddy. My baby picture on the cover. Holder of 15 medals and citations and can't recall for what. Received nine battle stars but only fired at tin cans. Invaded Korea with 13 bullets in my gun. Growing up in New York, gambling, subways, Times Square, school. Jobs in my lifetime: jockey, cook, telegram boy, Wall Street errand runner and bus boy at restaurants. Wounded in the Korean War, car accidents, broken back, brain concussion, broken ribs. My mother being left alone and never in school. She speaks broken English...*

I wondered why he had ended his notes there, and said, "I like your idea for a memoir," and turned away to hide my tears. Joe now waged a silent war against an internal enemy— cancer, a war he couldn't beat. Some days Joe seemed to rally, but the next day he was weak and confined to bed. I was powerless to help, especially now that I worked each day at the CBS news station, in the sales department on Sunset Boulevard. Although he was alone on certain days, I was grateful for the times Joe's friend John watched him for a few hours, whenever he could.

My friend Shelby, with other co-workers at CBS's sales department, arranged for a church volunteer to watch Joe for a few hours each day. Joe usually smoked in bed, and this upset me greatly, knowing he was on strong pain medication and could easily start a fire.

In order to keep my mind off Joe's deteriorating condition and ease my deep depression, I entered the employee CBS talent show at the urging of friends, and sang Roberta Flack's hit song, *Feel like Making Love*. I flubbed the second verse while trying to get my microphone cord untangled. Totally chagrined, I vowed never to sing in public again—only in the shower when no one could hear me.

A month later the CBS monthly newsletter was sent out to employees about the talent show, which included my photograph on the front page. The next day I received a call from the producers of the hit television sitcom *Rhoda,* starring Valerie Harper, to audition for a part. I was thrilled, but wondered why they failed to ask if I'd had any acting experience.

I arrived at the CBS Studio City lot where the producers of the show took one look at me and said, "You don't have the right look." I'm certain my lack of acting experience influenced their decision. Another producer went so far as to say I didn't even look like my photograph! Friends wondered why I didn't fib a little about my acting experience. They said everyone in Hollywood does it on their resume, but I couldn't lie. Obviously, I wasn't meant to sing or act.

A few days later my co-worker and friend Shelby invited me

to see a tea-leaf reader in the San Fernando Valley. I was hesitant to go until John offered again to watch Joe while I was out a few hours. Again, I felt the need to consult a psychic about my future, even though I was having dreams of Joe's death. My friend Shelby's husband, Bill, was a struggling musician, and I had always sensed that one day he'd be famous, and predicted his success on several occasions. That night, the tea leaf reader told Shelby that the tea leaves foretold of her husband's upcoming success. She could see him crowing about his accomplishments soon. Next the psychic peered into my tea cup and said, "I see a great loss in your life, and you will marry again, with the best relationship in your early fifties."

There's no way I'd remarry if Joe died, I thought.

In the following months my prediction and the tea-leaf reader's prediction for Shelby came true— her husband, Bill Conti went on to write the film score to the hit movie *Harry and Tonto,* starring Art Carney, that same year. In 1976, Bill was hired to compose the music for a small United Artists film called *Rocky,* and the rest is movie history. The song *Gonna Fly Now* from Rocky became a phenomenal success.

Bill Conti also conducted for the Academy Awards shows for many years, and also composed music scores for television and movies like the *Karate Kid, For Your Eyes Only,* and *The Thomas Crown Affair.* In 1983 he won an Oscar for the symphonic score for the movie *The Right Stuff.*

L to R: Shelby Conti and author Betsey Lewis
Reunion at Marina del Rey, California, 1982

Chapter Six
A Journey Ends

People face death in different ways. Some stay in denial, while others are depressed and retreat from the world. For Joe it was both.

Thanksgiving arrived and Joe's condition had deteriorated so much that he needed assistance to walk and eat. I called Joe's son Jack, a Marine, stationed near San Francisco and Joe's daughter Theresa in Wisconsin and suggested it was time to fly to L.A. and see their father. Joe's older daughter, Marsha, refused to fly to L.A. to see her dying father, feeling he abandoned her mother and siblings when they were children.

That first night Jack and Theresa talked to their father while I stepped into the bedroom to allow them their privacy. Theresa held her father's hand. "Daddy, I love you, you've got to return to the hospital where they can take better care for you." she said, and then added, "The doctors haven't been honest with you…you are dying."

I was surprised by Theresa's candid words, and even more surprised how Joe appeared relieved to finally hear the truth. The next day Theresa and Jack left and Joe returned to the Northridge Veteran's Hospital. After returning home from work that day I was stunned to find Joe home and in bed.

"What happened? I asked.

"They kicked me out," Joe said nearly in tears. "I refused to let them perform a liver biopsy when they know the cancer is in my liver."

I was furious, but also panic-stricken. He needed more care than I could offer. "Why would they do that?" I asked, and then kissed his forehead, the only place he didn't feel excruciating pain. Joe was curled up in a fetal position in bed, the flesh barely covering his emaciated body. It was unconscionable that the Veteran's Hospital could tell a dying veteran, a man who had served his country in both World War II and in Korea, to leave the hospital because he didn't submit to their excruciating tests. I had tried to hire a private nurse or get Hospice care, but the cost was more than we could afford. Mom wanted to watch Joe, but she worked full-time at a bank in Beverly Hills.

I picked up the phone and called John, Joe's best friend, and told him what had happened. John immediately placed a call to the hospital's administration and threatened to go to the media if Joe wasn't allowed to return to the hospital. The next day Joe was readmitted to the Veteran's Hospital in Northridge. Somehow without my knowledge or permission, doctors convinced Joe to submit to the painful biopsy, which only confirmed that his cancer had metastasized to his liver.

Despite my love for Joe, I couldn't bear to visit him each day and watch him suffer both in mind and body. The veins in his arms had collapsed from blood drawn from his arms, and now nurses poked needles in his leg veins to extract blood. Joe who once weighed 155-pounds, now weighed a gaunt 95-pounds, and loose skin hung from his skeletal frame. Each day I watched Joe die a slow death, and each day a part of me died with him.

Usually during visits I found Joe heavily sedated from morphine, which made him incoherent, or sleepy. I usually sat beside his bed and held his hand, whispering how much I loved him, and then returned home and prayed. As much as I believed in the afterlife and reincarnation, I was losing faith in my ability to reach God. Humans sometimes seem to be perpetuated in a victim consciousness, and at that time I felt that way. This belief has constantly cropped up in the readings I've given over the years—people believe they are helpless to change their lives, and that's exactly how I felt. Joe had created his cancer through his chain smoking, years of drinking, and poor eating habits. I also felt that Joe experienced extreme guilt for two failed marriages and the children he left behind. Our illnesses are dis-ease, and we create our illness when there are deep-seated emotional issues we haven't resolved through the years. We are born with free will and create our destiny—I knew this, yet I was caught in my own never-ending victim pattern, and so was Joe.

Each day Mom called to find out if there was anything she and Moe could do to help me. With only four days left until Christmas, she invited me for dinner that night, but I declined, sensing something was going to happen. As soon as I hung up with Mom, the phone rang again and a female voice asked if I was Joe's wife. She identified herself as Joe's doctor. I didn't wait for her to continue before asking, "What's wrong with Joe?"

"I'm afraid your husband has lapsed into a coma due to a blood clot in his lung. You need to get to the hospital right away." I phoned Mom back and explained Joe's condition, and then drove to the Veteran's Northridge Hospital in a thick, dream-like fog.

I rushed to Joe's room and found him lying in his hospital bed motionless, his face ashen, his fingernails blue and his breathing labored. A nurse forced a tube down his throat to drain the fluid filling his lungs, threatening to drown him. This was the first time I had witnessed the process of death. Death had a smell, a color and a sound. Each precious breath rattled inside Joe's chest. Memories raced through my mind, both good and bad, all the poignant life experiences we had gone through until that moment. Questions swirled in my head—did Joe ever love me? Did he come back into my life because he feared no one would care for him when he first learned of his illness?

The next morning a Catholic priest was summoned by John to administer the last rites to Joe. When the priest discovered Joe and I weren't married in the Catholic Church, he informed us the only way he'd perform last rites is if Joe renounced our marriage. I was stunned a priest of Roman Catholic Church could be so insensitive about our marriage and Joe's condition. How could a man in a comma renounce his marriage, and why should he even if he was alert?

John came to my rescue and caught the haughty priest by the arm and whispered something in his ear. The priest glared at John and then marched back into Joe's room to perform the last rites. I pulled John aside and asked, "What did you say to the priest?"

John gave me his impish smile and said, "I told him if he didn't give Joe his last rites, Joe might not be the only one meeting God today!" I had to laugh at New York John's brutally outspoken manner. While Joe's other so-called friends had vanished after they learned of his illness, John had stayed a steadfast friend.

Although Joe remained in a comma, I sensed he could hear my words as I repeated my love for him and told him to hang on a little longer because his son Jack was on the way to the hospital from San Francisco. As I spoke to Joe, I flashed back to the time I volunteered as a Candy Striper in Junior High at a local southern Idaho senior facility. An elderly woman named Nancy had suffered several strokes, and was unable to speak or eat by herself. My duty was to feed her each day. Although her face remained unresponsive I could tell she heard my words by the light in her eyes. I spoke her about death, about the afterlife and about love, and held her fragile hand each day. Like Nancy, I knew Joe's subconscious mind had heard my words.

At 3:26 p.m. Jack came running into Joe's room and I left the room. Within minutes Jack walked out of the room sobbing, and said his father had passed away. At age forty-night Joe had waited for Jack to arrive before taking his final breath at 3:30 p.m. that afternoon, December 22, 1974. I left the hospital in a daze and stood outside as cold Santa Ana winds gusted past me, reminding our time on this planet is gone before we know it. I was no longer the naïve twenty-four-year-old from Idaho—I had graduated to adulthood.

Emptiness and sadness became my constant companion. For three years I had been Joe's caregiver and the stress had taken its toll on me—I needed more time off. However, I returned to my CBS sales department job two days later, unable to take more time off to recover completely from Joe's death. I was overcome with emotion when Shelby Conti and my co-workers presented me with a large check from the sales department to help pay for Joe's funeral. The check was an unexpected surprise and much needed for Joe's costly funeral.

John made all the funeral arrangements for Joe's military funeral and burial at the National Veteran's Cemetery in West Los Angeles. It was a blessing to have such special friends during this time.

Three days later, on a bone-chilling rainy day, Joe was buried at the V.A. Cemetery. Words left unspoken, deeds left undone, and in an instant the flicker of life is gone. I studied the people at the cemetery and wondered what they were thinking: Joe's brother Danny from Salt Lake City; Joe's son Jack and his wife from San Francisco; Joe's ex-wife and daughter from Los Angeles, John, Joe's best friend, and Mom and Moe. Joe's mother Mary, in Miami, and his two sisters from New York were unable to attend the funeral service. Joe's eldest brother lived in England and had been estranged from the family for years.

After the eighteen-gun salute, two military officers picked up the American flag that was draped over Joe's wooden casket, folded it and presented to me. Bereft of tears at the moment, I clutched the flag to my breast as if holding a baby, and silently said my good-bye.

Shortly after Joe's death, Mom had a big argument with Moe and flew to Honolulu to visit relatives. I was invited to accompany her for an all-expense paid trip to Hawaii, but I declined—all my vacation time from work had been used up for Joe. The day Mom left, Moe phoned asking where she had gone. When I hesitated, he claimed he already knew where she had gone and had the number where she was staying in Honolulu. A few days later Moe flew to Hawaii where they reconciled. They stayed another week on the big island, enjoying the tropical paradise, while I realized I should have taken a much needed rest.

The death of a close family member or close friend is the hardest thing for most people to face. Everyone handles death in their own way. Some people are in shock or even denial, and others seem to be in a state of limbo for months. For me, even though I knew life continued after death, I really wasn't prepared for Joe's inevitable death. My world fell apart, and a great emptiness tore at my heart each day. Not even my belief in the spirit world and reincarnation seemed to fill the void. At night I cried, and at work I hid my pain.

As the days flew by I experienced nightmares of Joe's

appearance in his final days of life. I sensed he was trying to communicate with me, but he was still healing on the Other Side. Slowly the nightmares turned to pleasant dreams of a happy and healthy Joe. In one peculiar dream Joe phoned and said he had faked his death so I could be free again to pursue my life. This was Joe contacting telling me I was free to resume my life again and not feel guilty about it. This was the only spirit communication I received from Joe.

I had wanted to give psychic readings again for friends, but I was too depressed, stressed and worried about Joe's health and this made it impossible to connect with spirit. My only connection at that time to my spirit guides was through my vivid dreams and the times they called my name early in the morning.

Although my relationship to Joe was fleeting and strangely complicated and painful, our love produced the best gift that life had to offer, one that will last a lifetime—our beautiful and talented singer-songwriter daughter Camille Alvey. Perhaps we came together for a brief time to heal some karmic lesson from the past.

There were more tears and heartbreak to my story but I'll leave you with that for now. My relationship with my only child, my daughter Camille, has been as heartbreaking, joyful, tearful and strained as my relationship was with Joe. Sometimes it is impossible to have a meaningful relationship with certain family members—parents, siblings, children, no matter how hard we try to make it work and no matter how much we love them. It's best to let me grow and evolve in their own way, and send them love and prayers along their spiritual journey. It's called unconditional love!

Betsey and Joe's daughter, Camille Alvey

Chapter Seven
Remote Viewing

Remote viewing (RV) is the practice of projecting one's mind through time and space through extra-sensory perception (ESP). Remote viewing was popularized in the 1990s following the declassification of documents related to the Stargate Project, a $20 million dollar research and experiment program conducted by the U.S. Government, starting in 1975. The experiments were military applications pertaining to psychic phenomena.

Documents showed the project was terminated in 1995 when it failed to produce any useful intelligence information. Conspiracy buffs, however, believe to this day that government remote viewing experiments continue. I'm not a trained remote viewer, yet I've astral projected or remote viewed many places through the years. I inherited this gift from Mom, an amazing psychic.

There were times that Mom described what someone was doing from her astral view, and there were friends who attested to her being in two places at once. While we lived in Los Angeles, several friends in Idaho claimed they talked to her in person, but that was impossible because she was still in Los Angeles.

What is the difference between remote viewing and dreaming? Very little. Both involve projecting one's thoughts over time and space.

That's what happened to me in 1978. I woke from a life-like dream where men were seated in front of a large screen or monitor, viewing a desert-like surface. Although the images were shown in black and white, I sensed the surface color was red, and I was viewing the planet Mars. Here's where things got really weird—I stood inside the room with men, perhaps scientists and engineers, who appeared to be stunned by the images on the monitor. They patted each other on the back, unable to contain their excitement. Suddenly I was propelled to the surface of this rocky terrain where I noticed spiral formations, three-sided pyramidal structures and a gigantic ramp. A space probe orbited above me.

I later learned that Viking I and Viking II space probes landed on the surface of Mars in June and August of 1976, two years earlier than my dream. More than 4,000 photographs were returned from the Viking landers as well as 52,000 images from both orbiters. The Viking mission was designed to last for only 90 days, but stretched into years with the Viking I, with its final transmission on

Nov 11, 1982.

One of those images set the UFO community on fire, when the image of what looked like a humanoid face was sent back to Earth. The "Face of Mars", as it became known, was discovered on the Cydonian Mesa, situated at 40.75° north latitude and 9.46° west longitude. Near the Face were hills that resembled three-sided pyramids. Viking chief scientist Gerry Soffen dismissed the so-called "face" in image 35A72 as a trick of light and shadow, but Richard C. Hoagland, author and proponent of various conspiracy theories, believed the "face" to be proof of a long-lost Martian civilization.

Of course, NASA, after analysis of the higher resolution pictures from Mars Global Surveyor, stated that "a detailed analysis of multiple images of this feature revealed a natural-looking Martian hill whose illusory face-like appearance depends on the viewing angle and angle of the illumination."

I dismissed the dream until 1983 when artist friends invited me to a dinner party at their loft apartment in downtown Los Angeles. A NASA computer scientist named Frank was at the dinner party, so I jumped at the chance to question him about the Mars missions, wondering if there might be any credibility to my dream.

Frank slowly replied, as if contemplating his words, "How do you know about the ramp? Who told you?"

I explained how I had dreamed of a giant monitor that might have been at the Jet Propulsion Laboratory (JPL) in Pasadena, and witnessed what I thought was a real event, in real time. Finally he revealed that the Viking orbiters sent back photographs of a monolithic face, pyramidal shapes, a ramp formation and a formation he called the "Ram's Horn." Then he mysteriously cautioned me never to discuss our conversation about Mars.

I can't verify if Frank actually worked for NASA or if he was telling the truth about the anomalies on Mars, but I do know that my artist friends never heard from him again, which added to the mystery.

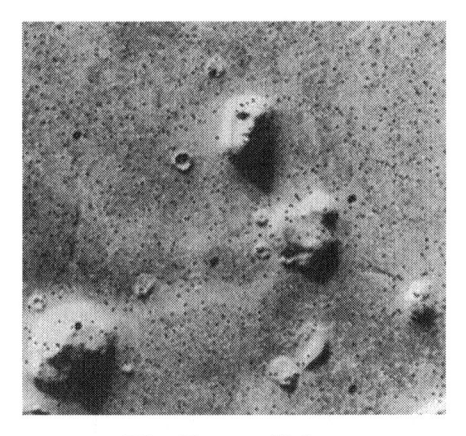

The Face of Mars

Chapter Eight
Reincarnation is Real

Through the years I've glimpsed past lives, including the past lives of friends, family and clients. In one of my visions I was a woman in a bonnet driving a covered wagon across the open plains with my small daughter by my side. My hands were weathered and looked much older than my true age from hard labor. The vision ended as I looked at a young girl, perhaps my daughter, fearing for her safety on the long trip to the West.

In a dream-like vision I was shown a young Indian boy riding his pony to escape the U.S. Calvary soldiers who were chasing him. I felt I was that Indian boy.

In another vision, I was shown ancient catacombs and then the vision switched to ancient Egypt, where I was a daughter of a pharaoh. Years ago a psychic confirmed my vision—I was one of many daughters of Ramesses II, son of Seti I, who reigned from 1279 B.C. to 1213 B.C. in the Ninetieth Dynasty. Ramesses was the pharaoh most responsible for erasing the Amarna Period from history. He defaced Amarna monuments and restored the belief in many gods of the priesthood, after Pharaoh Akhenaten had tried to bring about a one-god religion.

It's strange, but I've always admired the mysterious Pharaoh Akhenaten, known as a heretic, who for the first time in Egyptian history depicted wall art that showed human emotion. The remaining temples still show Akhenaten embracing with his beautiful wife Nefertiti and his children. His one-god religion was represented in the form of a solar disk.

I remember the first time I read a book about author and humorist, Mark Twain (1835-1910), I felt connected to him, as if I had known him during that era. There are things I've intuitively known about Mark Twain before reading about his adventures and his interest in time travel, science, his love of animals, especially cats, and his friendship with inventor Nikola Tesla. Many times I've found myself in tears whenever I read about him or looked at his photograph. Obviously there was a soul remembrance of Mark Twain for me, but I have no idea how I was acquainted with the famous author.

While working as a temporary secretary at a Hollywood talent agency, I met Diane, another temporary secretary. The talent agency on Sunset Boulevard represented clients like John Travolta, his brother Joey Travolta, Steve Martin and Rosanne Cash.

Diane was anxious for me to meet her friend Jean Lori, an aspiring actress, and hear about her past life story. As soon as I met Jean, I sensed she had been a famous actress in a past life, and mentioned it to her. She was amazed because she had an amazing story to tell me. Jean Lori recalled her life as 1930s actress and sex symbol Jean Harlow, known for her platinum-blonde hair, form-fitting white satin gowns, and pencil-thin arched eyebrows.

Our next meeting was at Jean's Studio City house, and again I was taken back by her stunning beauty. She stood nearly six-feet tall, her eyes were piercing brown and she had long dark-brown hair, nothing like the petite, blonde actress from the nineteen thirties.

Actress Jean Lori

Inside the house I sensed a spiritual presence and suddenly her kitchen light turned off and on by itself. Jean laughed and said it happened all the time, and then she poured out her story and past life as Jean Harlow.

She began, "Jean Harlow was born March 3, 1911, and I was born February 20; we were born under the astrological sign Pisces. Jean Harlow and I both married at sixteen and our marriages ended soon after, and we moved to Hollywood to get into the movies. And another thing…my mother and Jean Harlow's mother were both Christian Scientists."

Jean continued her story as I listened, spellbound. "Producer Marv Rothman knew Jean Harlow well and the first time he met me he was shocked that I walked like Jean Harlow, held my mouth like her, and had the same cry, and many of the same features. He was amazed that even my handwriting was the same."

Next, it was Diane's turn to explain. "Jean Harlow made movies with Laurel and Hardy, Clark Cable, William Powell and Spencer Tracy as the tough as nails, loaded with sex appeal dame. She died on June 7, 1937 at Cedar of Lebanon Hospital in Los Angeles from what was believed to be uremic poisoning at the age of twenty-six. There were rumors that the real cause of her death was from blows to her kidneys by her former husband and studio executive, Paul Bern, who committed suicide during their marriage."

1930s actress Jean Harlow

Jean explained she was recently regressed through hypnosis by well-known author and paranormal investigator Brad Steiger, and another hypnotist. She stated under hypnosis that she recalled how she had died as Jean Harlow and it wasn't from blows to her kidneys from her husband Paul Bern five years earlier. Her early death had sinister overtones involving a famous politician at the time and a murder of a world renowned man, and how she witnessed the murder of this man known to the entire world.

Jean Lori's Indian guru was Baba Muktananda, who she had met in New York City, her home town. She had spent considerable time with Baba, the founder of Siddha Yoga. Her house was full of photographs of her beloved guru. My sense was that Jean and Diane had an additional motive for inviting me to Jean's house, and it wasn't long before Diane confessed that they wanted my step uncle, William Peter Blatty, to help them get their book and movie launched.

I never approached Bill about Jean's story, knowing he was involved in directing *The Ninth Configuration,* based on his original novel, *Twinkle, Twinkle, Killer Kane.* I believed Jean's story of reincarnation, especially after producer Marv Rothman confirmed that Jean knew too many details about the 1930s actress that weren't known to the public. At the time my friend Dennis, who was a reporter for the National Enquirer, wanted an exclusive on Jean Lori's story. Jean interviewed with him and the story was set to go to press, but at the last minute Jean asked that the story be pulled from publication without any explanation.

Shortly after the National Enquirer fiasco, Jean and Diane went their separate ways. Jean eventually moved back to New York City, and Diane disappeared. Years later, a mutual friend said that he was on a flight with Jean to New York and she was doing well as an actress. She was on her way to New York for her beloved guru's funeral.

If Jean's story of Jean Harlow was true, and as Jean Harlow she had witnessed the assassination of a very famous person known to the world, it's probably one of the most shocking stories of our time. During my research into Jean's story of Jean Harlow I uncovered evidence about the politician and his corrupt dealings in the U.S. and Europe just before World War II, and how he was involved in the movie studios, and most likely, he had met or had been involved with Jean Harlow. Jean Lori did not have access to this information at the time of her hypnosis sessions.

Still, I'm left to wonder if Jean Lori was channeling Jean Harlow, a tormented soul, who may have been murdered for what she had witnessed in the basement of the prominent politician's home. Was Jean Lori really the reincarnation of Jean Harlow?

Unfortunately I'm not at liberty to divulge the entire story and the real names of the people involved due to the powerful status of this person and the lineage of his name, but perhaps in time others will come forward with the rest of the story.

I've always believed in reincarnation. There are countless stories of reincarnation worldwide, and especially in countries like India and Tibet. His Holiness the Dalai Lama, the 14th Dalai Lama, for example, was selected as the rebirth of the 13th Dalai Lama. To make this happen, a search party was sent to locate the new incarnation when the current Dalai Lama known as Lhamo or Thondup was two-years-old. It is said that among other omens, the head of the embalmed body of the thirteenth Dalai Lama which had been facing southeast, mysteriously turned to face the northeast, indicating the direction in which his successor would be found. The Regent, Reting Rinpoche, soon had a vision at the sacred lake of Lhamo La-tso indicating Amdo as the region where they would find a one-story house with distinctive guttering and tiling. After extensive searching, the Thondup house, with its features included in Reting's vision, was finally found. Thondup was presented with relics, including toys, that had belonged to the 13th Dalai Lama. It was reported that Thondup had correctly identified all the objects owned by the previous Dalai Lama and exclaimed, "It's mine! It's mine."

If we didn't have the ability to return to our physical bodies then how could we evolve as spiritual beings? I believe we can evolve on the Other Side, but not as quickly as we can in physical form. No one on Earth, as far as I know, is perfect, not even his Holiness the Dalai Lama, who readily admits this. We all need powerful lessons of love, compassion, and forgiveness. Reincarnation allows the soul to grow and mature and experience all the emotions of being human. After experiencing many visions of past incarnations, reincarnation makes perfect sense to me.

Chapter Nine
A Volcano Dream

In 1980 I moved to Portland, Oregon, and enrolled in the Community College for a writing class, and at the same time, Dad and my new stepmother moved to Salem, Oregon, from Idaho.
Probably one of the most unusual events of my life happened when I left from Portland on a Friday evening at 5:00pm to drive to my father's home in Salem. I called to let Dad know I was on my way, but as soon as I walked in the door he looked concerned and asked why it had taken me two hours to drive from Portland instead of the usual one hour.

I gave Dad a puzzled look. "What are you talking about?"

"It's after 7:00 o'clock," he said, pointing to the wall clock.

As incredible as it sounds, I don't know where I was during that missing hour. There were no accidents or heavy traffic to explain my missing hour.

May arrived and I was invited on a rafting trip on the upper Deschutes River. The weather had been great for experiencing Class II white water rapids and a few Class V rapids for the first time. It was an amazing experience, but shortly after the trip I had a haunting dream of a volcanic eruption.

In the dream I stood on a snowcapped mountain and heard its heartbeat. The sound came faster and faster until I lost my balance and slide down its side, feeling it bulge as if the mountain were about to give birth. Before I could run, the mountain exploded. A glowing substance raced down its sides, burying everything in its path. I woke sensing that the dream was either a warning of a cataclysmic event or a metaphor about my own turbulent life at the time.

When I returned from the rafting trip Dad called to tell me he dreamt of the Hawaiian Goddess of Fire, Pele. He didn't recall what she told him, but he said the dream seemed real. This was the first time Dad discussed his dreams. It had always been Mom who had talked freely about her psychic experiences.

On Sunday, May 18, 1980, at 8:32 a.m. Pacific Time when my dream became reality and Mount St. Helens, part of the Cascades in southwestern Washington, violently erupted after several weeks of rumblings. Gas and steam hurled rock and ash out across the land at speeds estimated at 670 miles per hour, obliterating everything in its path. The entire north face of the volcanic mountain, a half mile wide and about a mile from the peak to the base, collapsed and exploded with a force compared to a half dozen atomic bombs. A cloud of ash turned daylight into darkness in Yakima, and closed airports as far east as Missoula, Montana, almost five hundred miles downwind.

The collapse of the northern flank of St. Helens mixed with ice, snow, and water to create mudflows. The mud flowed many miles down the Toutle and Cowlitz Rivers, destroying bridges and lumber camps. A total of 3,900,000 cubic yards of material was transported 17 miles south into the Columbia River. Fifty people, including scientists, were killed instantly by the eruption, and millions of indigenous deer, 1,500 Roosevelt elk, 200 black bears and 15 mountain goats perished.

For more than nine hours a vigorous plume of ash erupted, eventually reaching 12 to 16 miles above sea level, creating its own electrical storm. The plume moved eastward at an average speed of 60 miles per hour with ash reaching as far as Idaho. Ash from the eruption collected on top of cars and roofs as far as the city of Edmonton in Alberta, Canada. A few days later a second eruption sent heavy gray ash over Portland, Oregon. Again, my spirit guides had warned me of a major event.

***

Anwar Sadat, President of Egypt, was known as the "Hero of the Crossing" because of his efforts to forge peace between Israel and Egypt. Israel eventually recognized Egypt as a formidable foe, and Egypt's renewed efforts led to the regaining and reopening of the Suez Canal through the peace process. I wasn't interested in

Mideast politics, but I was aware of Sadat, knowing he was not well-liked by many. As President, he led Egypt into the October War of 1973, to liberate Egypt's Sinai Peninsula which Israel had occupied since the Six-Day war of 1967. This had made him a hero in Egypt, and in the Arab world.

And then I had a dream so frightening and so vivid, I was convinced it was real. In the dream I was seated in a large theater filled with people. Suddenly, a man with eyes glaring with hate, jumped up in front of me and began shooting an assault rifle. Days later the assassination of Anwar Sadat was reported on October 6, 1981, during the annual victory parade held in Cairo to celebrate Egypt's crossing of the Suez Canal.

The assassin, Islambouli, emptied his assault rifle into Sadat while he sat in the stands, killing him instantly. In addition to Sadat, eleven others were killed, including the Cuban ambassador, an Omani general, a Coptic Orthodox bishop and Samir Helmy, the head of Egypt's Central Auditing Agency. Twenty-eight were wounded, including Vice President Hosni Mubarak, Irish Defense Minister James Tully, and four U.S. military liaison officers.

To this day I'll never forget that dream and how I was shown Sadat's assassination and the hatred in his killer's eyes. Although the event didn't happen inside a theater as I was shown in my dream, nonetheless, it took place during a parade where people were seated in an outdoor stand.

Sadat had been engaged in negotiations with Israel, which culminated in the Egypt-Israel Peace Treaty. This had won for him and Israel's Prime Minister Menachen Begin the Nobel Peace Prize.

This action had angered the country's Muslim Brotherhood and leftists, which brought about his assassination. With the exception of Sudan, the Arab world and the PLO strongly opposed Sadat's efforts to make peace with Israel.

Chapter Ten
Crossing Over

Mom and Moe had tried to reconcile their marriage many times, but even counseling couldn't help get past their differences. Mom couldn't take Moe's ravings and gambling habit, and Moe found mother obstinate and impatient. One year later, Mom divorced Moe and went to at a construction company in downtown Los Angeles, where she worked in the account receivables department. She met Lucky, a handsome American Italian, and fell in love with this dashing salesman. She felt one day they'd marry, and they did—one year later. She was the happiest I'd seen her in years, although I sensed that her happiness was short-lived.

For several consecutive mornings I awoke with the dreadful feeling that Lucky didn't have long to live. I found myself tearful each morning, but unable to recall the dream. Mom and I shared such strong telepathic powers that it was impossible to hide anything from each other, so I wasn't surprised when Mom asked, "Lucky doesn't have long to live, does he?"

I took a deep breath and told her the truth. "My spirit guides keep telling me through dreams that it will be soon. I'm so sorry, Mom," I said, hugging her.

Although Lucky had experienced a mild heart attack, he appeared to be in good health. Then one day he complained that he couldn't breathe and that his chest hurt. He was rushed to the hospital by ambulance. Hospital tests revealed the unthinkable—Lucky had lung cancer. We were devastated by the news.

Lucky was admitted into the hospital for chemotherapy and on the second day Mom called me from the hospital, "Lucky died from a massive heart attack." I was shocked that Lucky had died so quickly, even though my dream had warned me of his death. Lucky died one month after he and Mom had wed. A few weeks after Lucky passed away my father was rushed to the emergency room in Salem, Oregon, coughing up blood clots. One little melanoma cancer on his face had metastasized into pharyngeal cancer and he required radical surgery called laryngectomy to remove his larynx. At the same time, Moe had already informed us that he had pancreatic cancer.

I soon discovered information on a new cancer treatment called Catrix, which was a drug derived from bovine cartilage, deemed the new wonder cancer drug. Doctor John Prudden, a former associate professor of surgery at the College of Physicians and Surgeons of Columbia University and Presbyterian Hospital in New York, had developed the drug. I discovered a recommended physician in Sherman Oaks who treated patients with Catrix. He had been diagnosed with a cancer two years earlier and his cancer remained in remission. Finally, it seemed we had found a new cancer treatment that showed incredible promise. Moe started the treatment, and during the Thanksgiving holidays Dad drove to Los Angeles to begin the Catrix treatments, after going through surgery and radiation treatments.

It was strange hearing my father force air up to create an artificial-sounding voice, not the voice I had known all my life. The biggest shock was Dad's face and neck, now bloated almost beyond recognition from radiation treatments. There were small tumors that covered his back and neck.

We had a family reunion during the holiday—Mom was there, my sister Kathy and her husband Hector, Dad's brother and his wife, and my cousins, Mary and Martin. Dad and Mom actually spoke to each other, and I could tell by the way Dad's eyes lit up that he still loved Mom.

Eventually Dad gave up on the Catrix treatments as his conditioned worsened. I flew to Salem the week before Christmas after receiving an urgent call from my stepmother about Dad's condition. He now relied on a portable oxygen tank to breathe. Knowing the end was near, I hoped to have a heart to heart talk with him so we could make amends for all the hurt and unresolved animosity between us. I needed to bridge the years of painful memories in a short time, if only my stepmother would leave us for a few hours. All I wanted was my father's love, his acceptance and forgiveness before he died.

The next day, when my stepmother went to the pharmacy for Dad's pain medication, I decided to talk to him while I had his full attention. As I applied iodine to his chest and neck as he instructed to reduce the swelling from the huge tumors that covered his back and chest, I asked, "Dad, why do you still have such anger for Mom and me?"

"Your mother is worthless," he shot back, fighting to regain his breath. I was taken aback by his cutting words. I knew he was resentful, but hearing him say it sent a jolt through me. "Like me, Dad?" I asked and waited for his reply, but all I heard was the sound of his labored breathing.

I was devastated by his rejection and could no longer suppress my emotions as I stood behind him and burst into tears. "You have held onto your anger far too long and it's turned to cancer. Can't you see what has happened, Dad?" I waited for him to answer, but again, there was only stinging silence. "Please, can't we stop hurting each other?" I was about to walk away when his hand reach up for mine and he grasped it tightly. Then he whispered, "I love you," in what sounded like his normal voice.

Tears of love and a longing to change the past flowed from me. Why did he take all these years to show his love? Now he was dying and there were no second chances to heal the past. "I love you too," I managed, and then I reached around and hugged him. A wave of peace passed through me. Visions of the past, of my childhood flashed before me of a father who had no patience for my reading disability and my dyslexia.

I left Salem knowing I'd never see my father alive again. Dad passed away on January 20, 1985, at age fifty-nine. Although I had dreamt of my father's passing months before, I didn't forewarn Mom, knowing she had already endured far too much heartache after Lucky's sudden death. Shortly after Dad's passing Kathy and Hector began to get mysterious phone calls late at night. The phone rang twice exactly at 11:55, the exact time Dad had passed away in Oregon. Kathy called the phone company to complain, but they had no explanation for the mysterious calls. Dad, I believed, was reaching out from the Other Side to tell us he was watching over us.

I kept in touch with Moe, but Mom refused to see him again. Then one day he appeared at my doorstep. "Your mother is a sick woman and needs my help," he said on the verge of guffaw. Although Mom loved Moe, she felt she had gone through enough since Lucky's death.

In some ways Mom and Moe shared similar dysfunctional childhoods, but there were major differences: Moe was born in Lebanon, abandoned by his father and raised by his immigrant mother in New York City along with his four siblings, while Mom was adopted at age five, and taken away from her four siblings and parents and placed in a foster home with a family in Idaho where she learned the candy business. At eighteen, she ran away from home and enlisted in the Navy. Perhaps it was their childhood abandonment that brought them together.

Days later Moe invited my husband and me to dinner at an Italian restaurant in the Sherman Oaks. That night Moe informed us he was staying in Bill's Beverly Hills guesthouse temporarily until he could find an assisted living home. Bill had recently married Julie, a former Los Angeles Rams football cheerleader, and they now lived in a luxurious Coldwater Canyon home. This was Bill's fourth marriage.

Moe talked about Bill's beautiful guest house and then he asked about Mom. Finally, his real motive for the dinner was revealed. He wondered if Mom would see him again and join him for dinner. I agreed to talk to her the next day and get back to him.

Mom surprised me and agreed to have dinner with Moe that weekend, so I drove Mom to Beverly Hills to pick up Moe at his brother's beautiful house on Coldwater Canyon. Moe greeted us outside Bill's home and insisted we say hello to Bill and his new wife Julie. I sensed something troubled Moe, and that's why he wanted to see Mom again.

"Bill and Julie are moving to Connecticut soon. They want me to join them there but I said no. I don't want to be a burden them. I'm going to check into a retirement home." He grew serious, his face drained of color. "Now my brother Eddie has pancreatic cancer." Moe seemed softer now, and more at peace. Even the loud booming voice was gone, even when he announced his cryptic, "We're doomed! We're doomed!"

"Is the Catrix helping?" I asked.

"Look at me," he laughed. "I look great." Moe was referring to the weight he had lost.

Mom and Moe talked on the phone daily and went out to dinner two more times, but Moe grew weaker each day, and found it difficult to drive from Santa Monica where he had moved into a senior care facility to the San Fernando Valley.

One day Moe appeared at my house door and barged through the foyer, stopping long enough to allow me to kiss his cheek. I could tell he was upset as he shoved a hundred dollar bill at me. "The Catrix didn't work so I sold all my stock," he said, looking jaundiced and thin. "I'm being admitted into the Santa Monica hospital tomorrow."

Moe discussed Bill and Julie, his occasional visits to their Beverly Hills home and how another doctor wanted to run more tests. He had refused their tests. Finally he offered his condolences about my father's passing in January.

"What did your doctor say about the cancer?" I asked.

"Ah, they're all a bunch of damned amateurs. Now my doctor claims the cancer is in my liver." I sensed Moe had accepted his terminal illness after his brother Eddie had died from the pancreatic cancer the month before. Bill and Julie were still preparing to move to Connecticut and insisting Moe join them, but again he refused, sensing his time was short.

The next day Moe called from the retirement home. "How are you?" he said, his words strangely slurred.

"Are you all right?" I asked, sensing something terribly wrong from his voice.

"I'm fine, just a little groggy," he replied.

I continued to question him, sensing an urgency to rush to

Santa Monica and check on him. "Why aren't you in the hospital?"

He jokingly answered, "They didn't want me."

Had he taken any medication, I asked. "No," he said. Did he want any help? Again, he said no. After I hung up, I jumped in my car and drove as fast as I could on the 405 Freeway from North Hollywood to Santa Monica. I parked in front of the retirement home and raced inside, searching for Moe's room, and found his door ajar. Once my eyes tried to adjust to the dimly lit room I found Moe lying on the bed, seemingly lifeless. My heart sank as I moved closer, and then I saw Bill standing by the window and Julie next to his bed.

"Is he alive?" I questioned Julie.

She nodded yes.

I stepped closer to Moe and found him barely breathing. Since he was wearing only his underwear, I dressed him in a robe and wiped his face with a damp cloth, waiting for the ambulance to arrive. Bill continued to stare out the window and Julie stood by Moe's bed.

The ambulance took Moe and I followed them to the hospital and stayed for an hour, awaiting word on his condition. The nurse said it would take time to evaluate him and suggested that we go home. I left Bill and Julie in the waiting room, and returned home, unable to accept my stepfather was dying.

The next morning I returned to the Santa Monica Hospital and found Moe alert, teasing the nurses, and insisting the doctors were a bunch of amateurs, as morphine dripped into his arm. Bill and Julie were seated across from his bed.

Moe looked at Bill, and with his off-beat sense of humor

said, "The devil is going to get me." I assumed the morphine was speaking. Then he turned to me and said, "Now I know, life is so simple...so very simple." Moe, I believed, in his final hours of life, had discovered a great truth about life: appreciate the simple things in life while you can.

Moe then grabbed my hand. "Don't go. I want you to stay," he said, fighting to keep his eyes open, and then he whispered to me as I kissed his forehead, "Pray for me."

"I love you, Moe and will pray for you. I'll see you tomorrow," I said, before leaving.

The next morning, I returned to the hospital and stopped at the nurses' station to inquire about Moe's condition. The nurse grimaced and said, "I'm so sorry...Mr. Blatty slipped away peacefully a half hour ago." I stood there in a daze, tears running down my cheeks, unable to comprehend that both my father and stepfather had died within three months of each other.

There was a small service held for Moe at the Beverly Hills Good Shepherd Catholic Church in Beverly Hills. Mother and I attended, and talked to Bill and his wife Julie outside the church. Bill sensed Moe was there listening to his eulogy.

Following Moe's death I dreamt of him constantly. In one really weird dream Mom and I were at a restaurant when we spotted Bill and Julie at a table. We started to be seated when Moe appeared, holding his head in his arms and laughing. Even in my dreams Moe's deadpan humor (no pun intended) came through. I missed him, his jokes and his constant complaints, "We're doomed!" or "Disaster!"

In another dream I floated adrift on the ocean in a small boat that brought me to Bill's home in Beverly Hills. I was discussing Bill's novel *The Exorcist* with a friend when Moe suddenly appeared. I was shocked to see him alive, and asked him how it was possible that he was alive. He replied, "I've been taking aluminum and it brought me back to life." I held his hand in the dream and said, "Moe, I wrote a book and you're in it."

He smiled and said, "I know!"

I believed Moe had actually visited me from the spirit world and wanted me to know he existed, surrounded by light (aluminum) from the Other Side. Moe was a dichotomy of magnanimousness and vindictiveness, yet I loved him for the kindness he had shown Joe and for the time he helped me during a difficult time in my life. During that time I had gotten involved with unscrupulous people in Los Angeles and lost a large sum of money because of their drug habit. Moe, like a father, let me stay at his apartment and gave me enough money to return to Idaho.

I had prayed for a sign from spirit to help Mom with her sadness and that day arrived on August 7 (another 7) as Mom and I unloaded groceries from the car trunk at one o'clock in the afternoon. It was a hot day in Los Angeles as cumulus clouds shed ice trail crystals across the sky like angel's wings. Suddenly I noticed a peculiar rainbow band overhead and behind the band of colors was a really odd cigar-shaped cloud. The band contained four luminous colors: red at the top, followed by yellow and purple, with a brilliant blue at the bottom. Oddly, the purple band had a huge hole in it that appeared to be a giant eye.

One by one each color dripped into the color below it, and each one faded and then grew brilliant again. I ran into the house and called a friend who worked in downtown Los Angeles, asking him to look in the sky for a rainbow band. He reported there was nothing unusual in the sky from his vantage point. I returned to Mom and we stood spellbound for half an hour as the colors melted two more times, grew radiant again, and then faded one by one. Just when I thought the vision was over, the iridescent blue at the bottom dripped down on the right side and turned luminous white, then shot to the East.

Oddly, nothing had been reported in the news about the meteorological anomaly, so I contacted a professor at UCLA meteorology department and asked if he had any explanation for our rainbow vision. He suggested it was a sundog, the phenomenon created when sunbeams are bent and reflected by ice crystals hanging in the air. However, he was perplexed by the 30-minute duration and the way the blue band turned brilliant white and shot off toward the East. He had no logical explanation for that. I concluded that Mom and I were given a special sign from spirit that Moe, my father and Lucky were at peace on the Other Side.

As time went by Mom's depression returned. The death of three former husbands within two years was more than devastating—it began to affect her health. This was the beginning of her deep depression and heavy drinking. She had recently talked about death and how she'd never incarnate on Earth again, but I always reminded her that we will all reincarnate again until we've learned our soul lessons.

So when Kathy and Hector moved from Los Angeles to Bear Valley outside the town of Tehachapi, California, in 1995, and offered to let mom stay at their ranch home, I was thrilled. I felt the move to Southern California might brighten her mood and give her the will to live again. I was wrong. Several months after the move Mom's beloved Siamese cat Sumac was hit by a car. Not long after her cat was killed, she suffered a mild heart attack. Mom's doctor warned her that she must stop drinking and smoking if she wanted to live longer. The warning scared her enough to quit her bad habits, but I knew that it was too late to reverse all the years she had neglected her health.

January rolled around and Kathy's husband Hector had contracted viral pneumonia and was at home in Tehachapi, recovering. Mom caught the highly contagious pneumonia and became very ill. She was admitted to the Bakersfield Hospital, approximately 45 miles from Kathy and Hector's home in Bear Valley. Kathy could only visit Mom once a week because she had six horses to care for as well as other pets, both a dog and cats. Mom's condition was serious, she told me. Immediately I booked a flight from Boise, Idaho, to Burbank.

While on the flight I sat beside two Buddhist monks who didn't speak English but smiled when they noticed I was reading the biography of Krishnamurti. They smiled and showed me their book on Buddha's teachings, and it was then I knew they were like guardians angels, there to comfort me in my time of grief. I also had another surprise on that flight. Former lead singer for Paul Revere and the Raiders, Mark Lindsay, and his wife sat behind me. I didn't want to intrude on their privacy, so I didn't speak to them, but thought it was coincidental that we were on the same flight to Burbank.

At the Burbank airport I rented a car and drove to Bear Valley to see Kathy before heading to the Bakersfield Hospital. There I found Mom curled up in a fetal position on a gurney in the hallway, waiting for a nurse to give her a new room. I was horrified by her condition. She was skeletal-looking, skin hung from her face and body. I hardly recognized my once-beautiful mother.

Mom opened her eyes as I approached her and whispered, "Thank goodness, J.R., you're here." Mom preferred to call me "Junior" or "J.R" instead of my given name. I leaned down and gently kissed her forehead, unable to hold back my tears. I could tell the hospital staff had neglected her and I was angry.

"Don't cry," she whispered.

Finally, a nurse wheeled her into a private room where I bathed her and dressed her in new pajamas. I held her hand, and told her how much I loved and missed her.

The next day, I returned to the hospital and applied Reiki energy on her for nearly two hours. In the following three days she appeared to improve and on the fourth day she convinced her doctor she was well enough to go home. On the drive back to Bear Valley Mom was quiet. Suddenly she said, "Remember that dream I had in which I kept typing the letter "P" over and over on a typewriter?"

"I remember your dream," I said.

"The letter "P" stood for pneumonia. The dream meant I'd get pneumonia." The moment Mom made the connection, I realized she had been given a warning about her health, and yet she ignored it. "You haven't given up, have you?" I asked, my heart breaking as I held her frail hand, noting arthritis had gnarled the little finger on her left hand.

"No…no," she replied and turned away to hide the truth.

"Please don't give up, Mom. I love you," I said, and reminded her that I planned to move back to Southern California and we'd visit Will Roger's beach, like old times.

Mom and I had spent many weekends at Will Rogers Beach when we had first moved to Los Angeles, sunbathing in the warm California sun, swimming in the ocean, and talking about our dreams. Our favorite song through the years had been, Our Day Will Come, a 1963 hit by Ruby and the Romantics, and we had believed our day would come. For Mom, however, her dreams would never be fulfilled.

"Sure, we'll go to the beach again," she said, and gave me her mysterious it will never happen smile. "Look at me, I'm a bag of bones," she managed, with a slight chuckle. I noted that the light that once shone in her beautiful sky-blue eyes, or corn-flower blue as she always described them, had dulled. I had seen the glimmer of light fade from Moe's and my father's eyes before their deaths. What saddened me most was Mom had given up the will to live and I selfishly didn't want to lose my best friend.

I began to sob as Mom patted my hand and said, "Please don't cry, J.R., everything will be all right."

Mom was still the wounded, adopted child, abandoned by her parents during the Great Depression, and I wanted to take all that pain and unhappiness away from her life. Many times she had told me that she'd never reincarnate again on this planet, there was too much pain here. I knew someday she'd return, despite her protests.

That night I stood on Kathy's porch, facing west one night and spotted comet Hale-Bopp lancing the sky. It was there to take Mom away to a wonderful place in the heavens.

Again I offered Mom more Reiki energy but she refused. It was obvious that she had allowed me to give her enough energy to leave the hospital, and now she was ready to die. I was upset. I didn't want to let her go. I flew back to Idaho the next day and to my job in Ketchum. While grocery shopping that evening I stopped in the middle of an aisle, sensing an urgent psychic message. I felt extreme pressure on my left hand, and glanced down to see that my hand had transformed into my Mom's arthritic left hand. The vision lasted only seconds, yet I knew Mom's soul had gone through me. She was there at that moment to say goodbye, and reassure me that it was her time to go, and for me to accept it. Knowing Mom's ability to astral project, I sensed she was there, especially when I realized my left hand had transformed into hers, the hand I'd held the day I drove her home from the hospital.

Mom's psychic ability was amazing. After my paternal grandmother died, when I was twelve-years-old, everyone had searched for a gold and pearl ring my grandfather had given her years before. They searched for days but the ring had simply vanished. Then one day as Mom and my aunt were dumping toiletries from her bathroom, Mom psychically felt she should dump out her body powder, and out fell the ring. There were many other instances of her psychic and telepathic ability, especially when we needed to communicate silently. We were kindred spirits. Oddly, Kathy never had that connection with Mom.

When Monday arrived I felt uneasy after the vision and kept calling Kathy to find out about Mom's condition. Each time Kathy reassured me that Mom was asleep and resting comfortably. My restlessness continued through the next morning. I woke at 2:36 a.m. and again at 3:26 a.m. Each of these times totaled the number eleven, which was the day Mom was born. Finally, I drifted off to sleep and dreamed.

In the dream I slept beside three relatives, and woke to see a dark, whirling cloud in the hallway. I got out of bed and went to the cloud in the hall, where a huge owl was sitting. It stared into my soul and spoke telepathically, "Don't be frightened." The owl then flew down a flight of stairs and managed to squeeze through a closed window vanishing from sight. At 5:04 a.m. I woke to hear a female voice whisper my name, and realized my spirit guides were there to forewarn of Mom's passing.

The dream unnerved me, knowing owls are harbingers of death. Blue birds are also known to be messengers of death, and I had seen a blue bird before Joe, my father and Moe had crossed over to the Other Side. Recently, a blue bird had flown into my yard.

Dreams are doorways to other realities. Each night we experience death and astral travel as we access many realities and many entities. I had read long ago that a dream can actually form the future. We form events, not realizing that their origins happened during sleep time.

Tuesday, February 11, arrived, and my uneasiness continued. The phone rang at ten o'clock that night and I knew it was Kathy calling about Mom.

"Mom has suffered a massive heart attack and was rushed to the local hospital by ambulance a few minutes ago. I'm headed to the hospital now," she said.

At exactly eleven o'clock Kathy called back to say Mom had lingered in a coma for one hour and died without regaining consciousness. I found it beyond coincidence that Mom was born on September 11, a day that would go down in infamy after the terrorist attack on the World Trade Center in New York City. Mom was born on the eleventh and died on February eleventh at eleven o'clock at night. I have no doubt she planned it that way.

I think most of us take our parents for granted until they become ill or leave us in death. For me, I always believed my mother would be there for me forever, and now her physical being was gone. Yet, I knew that death wasn't the end and that her essence was near, touching me when I heard her favorite songs or smelled her favorite perfume. Each time I'd visit Idaho's Sawtooth Mountains, Mom's beloved mountains, I feel her spirit in the wind, the river and the mountain lakes.

I returned to Tehachapi a week later to help Kathy with the funeral arrangements and decided to stay for a while. While going through Mom's belongings we discovered a note, undated, perhaps written months before. *From the beginning I was born in Ontario, Oregon on September 11, 1924. My father, Joseph, listed me on my birth certificate as Ella Ida, but my mother, Winnie, wanted me* called Ester Fay, and she won. I had four other siblings, Lillian, Hazel, Stella, and Sidney. Father was born in Kansas and he was 37, and my mother was born in Colorado and was 35 at the time of my birth.

By 1929, at the age of four I was placed in The Children's Home, an orphanage in Boise, Idaho, along with my sisters and brother.

The first time I was adopted, I was badly abused and the authorities took me back to the Children's home. The second adoption I was sent to live with a family in Twin Falls. My name was then changed to Bette Jane.

I joined the U.S. Navy and trained at Hunter's College in New York from 1944 to 1945. Later I was stationed at Treasure Island near San Francisco where I received an Honorable Discharge in 1946. My rank upon leaving the service was Storekeeper Third Class.

I wish to be cremated. I do not wish to be put on life support—no drugs—no service.
At the bottom of the note was a drawing, like a cat in the clouds. Next to the drawing Mom wrote, "Sumac and I are again together on that big white cloud," referring to her Siamese cat, killed months earlier by a car.

I puzzled over her child-like drawing of a cat in the clouds, recalling how Mom was an excellent artist who had taken commercial art classes at the University of Idaho. It seemed she had planned her death months earlier.

Kathy and I honored Mom's wishes to be cremated. We

arranged that she would be cremated three days later.

According to several metaphysical books I had read, our guardian angels or spirit guides need time to gather a person's soul records from their body. The eyes, the cells, the blood and the bones hold soul patterns, which are gathered and returned to the spiritual plane. If a person dies suddenly the records are still gathered but the process takes slightly longer.

Kathy kept Mom's ashes, with the plan to eventually visit Idaho and scatter them near Red Fish Lake, in the Sawtooth Mountains of Idaho, as Mom had always wished. That plan never happened.

Back in Idaho I experienced strange dreams about Mom. In one peculiar dream Mom was fully dressed, standing in the ocean, waving to me, but I sensed danger as large ocean waves rolled in. I warned her not to get too close, but she ignored me and dove into the waves. A man on shore spotted her and pulled her from the riptide. Back on shore, she was fine.

Kathy also experienced a strange dream, and called to tell me about it. "Mother was dressed in a pink robe. I hugged her, sensing an angel nearby, and then the angel whispered to me, 'Kay is going to take over now.'"

We both agreed Mom was trying to communicate to us, but who was Kay? Kathy suggested I stay with her in Tehachapi for a few months, but I had a great job at a furniture/design store in Sun Valley, Idaho, and didn't want to lose it.

Months later I found myself in financial problems from a bad investment and in deep depression over Mom's death. At the time my Guides tried to warn me not to get involved in the business venture with an Australian couple, but I ignored the gut-wrenching feeling and paid dearly for it. One day, as I was driving through a mountain pass, feeling really depressed by Mom's death and my financial loss, my SUV swerved sharply and I lost control. I nearly drove off a steep embankment. I stopped the car and sat there, shaken that I subconsciously wanted to end my life.

As I wept a strange feeling overwhelmed me, as I felt a feather-like tingling on the left side of my cheek. And then I heard Mom's voice inside my head say, "J.R., you have much more to do. Believe in yourself." No doubt she was there to guide and comfort me, and tell me that it wasn't my time to cross over to the Other Side. Suicide was a selfish act. I chose this life and, no matter what events unfolded, I needed to live it out. No more self-pity, I had a wonderful life to live.

The feather-like sensation on my cheek lasted many months. Then, one day, I had an overwhelming sense to write, my fingers racing across the paper, guided by an invisible presence. This is what poured from my fingers that day.

Dear J. R.,

I am sorry, my daughter, that in the ten years before my death, my alcoholism pushed you away from me. I had such anger and bitterness and such pain. I let those feelings hurt those closest to me. I know I hurt you and your sister Kathy and also my granddaughter Camille. I know you wanted me to be a loving grandparent and great grandparent, but how could I be when I never knew love as a child? Forgive me.

You were my sensitive child and I was closer to you than Kathy because of your sensitivity. I loved Kathy as much but in a different way.

I'm sorry your father and I never gave you and Kathy a happy and loving home as children. I watched as you, the eldest child, tried to be an adult, the healer and caregiver in the family during our violent fights. You took so much on your shoulders. What a burden for someone so young and sensitive.

I know you have had your moments of depression and great disappointments in people, but I'm proud you pulled through and never took your own life. You are like me, J.R., a chip off the old block.

Do not allow the disappointments and the harshness of life to harden you and turn you into a bitter old woman. Live for the moment and bless the goodness in your life. Do not chastise yourself for the past—it's done and gone and there's no looking back. Know you have done much to help others. I'm proud of you and know I watch over you always. With love forever, Mom

They say that when someone dies there is a birth in the family, and by the end of February my daughter, Camille, called to say that she was pregnant with her fifth child. I predicted this: "You will have another daughter with blonde hair and incredible blue-green eyes. Your grandmother is going to reincarnate as your daughter."

Camille laughed. She didn't take me seriously until she gave birth to a beautiful baby girl with light blonde hair and pale blue-green eyes on October 6. Camille named her Alexis Kay. Kathy's dream after Mom died, about an angel telling her "Kay was going to take over", had proven true. The first time I held Alexis Kay I was struck by her stunning turquoise eyes, reminding me of the opal earrings I had given Mom for her birthday the year before her death. I recognized the light in her eyes: it was Mom staring back at me through the windows of her soul.

As Alexis grew older, more and more similarities began to appear that reminded me of Mom. Alexis loved spaghetti like Mom, and she suddenly began collecting all kinds of Betty Boop memorabilia like Mom. For years Mom collected Betty Boop cartoon memorabilia, and her friends even nicknamed her Betty Boop, because of her delightful sense of humor.

You could chalk this all up to coincidence, but as you've probably guessed by now, I don't believe in coincidences. My granddaughter, now a teenager, is a very independent young lady with strong opinions like my mother. Can I say for certain Mom reincarnated as my granddaughter? No. I'll just have to trust my intuition that Mom changed her mind that Earth wasn't for her again, and returned as my granddaughter. However, there's one consolation for me: if Mom did return as my granddaughter, she is with a family that loves and cherishes her. No longer will she be the abandoned, wounded child, and that gives me great joy and peace.

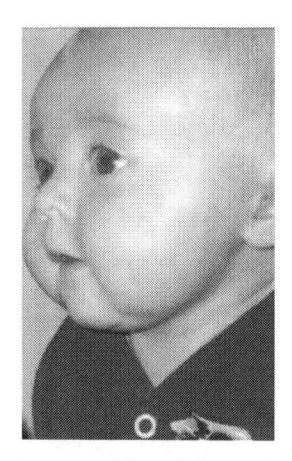

Author's granddaughter Alexis Kay

Author's mom, Bette

Chapter Eleven
Learning Indigenous Ways

Belize was far more beautiful than I had ever imagined. The moment I stepped off the plane with my friend, Michael, and I felt connected to the country, almost as if we had lived there in another lifetime.

As we drove through the lush green countryside in Central America, I was engulfed in feelings of déjà vu. We continued along dirt roads to the western border of Belize, where a large portion of precious rainforests had been cleared for lumber or burned to plant citrus groves. It saddened me greatly to see such destruction of valuable trees.

At that time Michael Jackson's *Earth Song* video had just been released. The video depicted rainforests totally destroyed, which actually took place within a week of the video shoot. The video also depicted animals slaughtered in Africa, but of course, no animal or human was injured for the video production. Before the video ends there's a scene where Earth is renewed and all life returns again, an event I've always sensed from early childhood. I wondered if Michael Jackson also felt a cleansing of Earth would take place and the rebirth of a new world. Indigenous all over the world foresee a time when the fourth world will be cleansed and those who survive will have another chance in the fifth world.

Michael's video resonated with me about the way humanity had forgotten how to love and honor all life, as indigenous peoples have understood. Everything on planet Earth has a consciousness which modern humans have forgotten. Sadly, rainforests and creatures are vanishing at an unprecedented rate.

My friend Michael and I drove to the village of San Jose Succotz. It was six in the evening, too late to take a ferry to the Mayan temples of Xanantunich. Michael tried to persuade the ferry owner to take us across the river to the Other Side, but he steadfastly refused. Finally, the man suggested that we swim across the Mopas River if we were that determined. So we swam across the murky river. All the while I worried that alligators or deadly fer-de-lance snakes lurked nearby. We reached the bank safely, however, and hiked a mile until we reached the towering Mayan temples. Dogs barked in the distance as we climbed to the top of a temple. Within minutes, two men bearing machetes appeared at the top of the temple with us.

Temples of Xanantunich

I froze in terror, recalling news that two tourists were murdered in Belize a few weeks earlier. Michael spoke Spanish to the men and the older man replied in English, "I'm the caretaker. What are you doing here so late, amigos?"

Michael explained how we'd missed the last ferry and decided to swim the river to explore the ancient courtyard. The caretaker laughed and offered to give us a tour of the grounds.
"This is the largest ceremonial center in the Belize River Valley, and we are standing on El Castillo, or the Castle, one hundred thirty feet above the plaza. There are six major plazas, surrounded by twenty-five palace structures," he explained.

"It's a mystery how the Mayan people built these great structures," I said.

"My people have a legend that our ancestors made rocks float in the air like magic."

I was shocked to learn the Maya people believe their ancestors had the ability to lift tons of rock through advanced levitation technology. There are theories that the ancient Egyptians built their pyramids with the use of levitation, and if so, it seemed as if ancient Maya had the same advanced techniques as ancient Egyptians. According to records the Mayan civilization lasted for more than 2,000 years. During the period from about 300 A.D. to 900 A.D., known as the Classic Period, these people made great progress in agriculture, astronomy and mathematics, and created an advanced calendar.

There are theories that ancient civilizations were given advanced technology by ancient aliens to create monolithic structures weighing tons. The ancient structures are found worldwide.

Late that evening, Michael and I arrived at the Jaguar Reserve and stayed in a small cabin furnished only with two small beds covered in mosquito nets. The following night we toured the rain forest with a group of people, an enchanting and magical place filled with the sounds of tropical birds, frogs, and the glimmer of dancing fireflies. Most intriguing of all was a fungus that possessed bioluminescent properties that glowed in the dark.

Author at Belize Jaguar Reserve in Belize

The next day we drove to an abandoned shrimp farm where Michael had once worked and made friends with the caretakers of the property, an Indian family. They were gracious people who didn't have much, but offered us a meal of rice and beans. We shared our cocoa with them – all we had to offer in return for their kindness. We spent the night in the abandoned shrimp farm building, listening to the wind moan under the metal roof.

Morning dawned and we drove to a blue water hole, a deep cavern filled with spring water and tiny fish. On the third day, we chartered a small plane to Ambergris Caye, an Island only 25 miles long, off the coast of Belize, where we spent one week snorkeling and scuba diving near the coral reef. The ocean was clear and filled with rainbow-colored fish, enormous grouper, graceful manta rays, and menacing barracuda. Each day I prayed to the water spirits for protection, believing that everything in our world has a consciousness, and if I honored that consciousness, I'd be protected.

Michael, being an adventurous soul, rented a small wooden sail boat, which was fine, except it appeared to need major repairs. My intuition warned me not to go, but I'm not always a good listener! Strong winds carried us out several miles from shore late that balmy afternoon, and then it happened—we heard a loud boom as the main sail snapped in half. How would we get back?

Now the sun was quickly dipping into the West, and the wind was only a gentle breeze, rocking us on the ocean as the currents pulled us further out to sea.

Ambergris Caye off the coast of Belize

To make matters worse, the boat had no motor, no oars, and no lights of any kind to signal our distress. Our only companions were hundreds of large cockroaches swarming from the floorboards to escape the water slowly seeping into the boat! Although Michael remained calm, I knew we were in a precarious and very dangerous situation. There was no one knew we were gone, and the owner, a somewhat shady character, probably didn't care after getting our money. He had convinced us the boat was sea worthy. We'd be invisible, bobbing in the ocean in the pitch blackness of night until the boat sank into the ocean.

Luckily, the jib sail was intact, and all we needed was wind to get us back to shore. That's when I prayed to my spirit guides to get us back safely to land. Suddenly, a breeze stirred, and Michael adjusted the rigging below the small torn sail, turning the boat toward shore. Three hours later we arrived back at shore, with help from my unseen friends. It was an adventure I'd never forget or want to repeat again.

We also ventured deep into the rainforest to meet with a Maya medicine woman who had prepared an herbal mixture to take back to a friend, Steve, who was battling lung cancer. The medicine woman burned sweet amber and spoke as if in a trance. "Take this medicine to your friend and have him take this medicine each day. He is not good," she said in her Spanish accent. We paid her and left with the herbal medicine. Upon our return to Idaho we discovered our friend had taken a turn for the worse and was in the hospital. We were unable to deliver the herbs, and one month later Steve passed away from the cancer.

Visiting Belize made me long for a simpler life like that of the people we met in the countryside. One year later, I returned with Michael to Belize. On this trip I learned a powerful lesson about honoring sacred sites. We stopped at the Altun Ha temple, a few miles from Belize City, on our way to the airport at the end of our trip. We climbed the largest structure, known as The Temple of the Masonry Altars, which rose 60 feet above the plaza. According to the guide, human and animal sacrifices had been conducted on altars in the area. As we walked around the ancient plaza, I spotted another altar at ground level and climbed on it, asking Michael to take my picture.

Although I said several prayers for protection before hopping up on the altar for a photo, I felt uneasy about it. Michael snapped the picture and we returned to our rental car.

Maya altar near the Temple of Altun-Ha

Author at Temple of Altun-Ha

Back in the car I doubled over in excruciating pain. It felt as if a dagger had been thrust into my stomach. The moment the pain hit, I knew that I had dishonored the ancient spirits who resided at Altun Ha, and began to pray aloud, "I'm sorry for offending you. Please stop the pain," and the pain abruptly stopped at that instant.

The spirits at Altun Ha had taught me an important lesson that day about respecting sacred sites and the spirit ancestors who still dwell there. Theories suggest that if a person passes over suddenly, or a group of people die together from violence, their energy will linger in the physical world for an eternity or until that soul or souls realizes that love will embrace them if they cross over into the light. Other theories suggest that residual negative energy is locked into stone.

As an empath I must have felt the tragic killings that had taken place there centuries before, or I encountered an intelligence who was angered by my frivolity until voiced my regret. The spirits there were angered until I apologized and showed my reverence to them. There are places around the world and stories of people who have taken rocks or other items from sacred sites and paid dearly for it. The post office can attest to the hundreds of rocks returned to Hawaii each year.

***

My spiritual path turned to the Native American beliefs and began attending sweat lodge ceremonies, pow wows and vision quests. Through the years I have studied many religions and attended a variety of churches, but nothing felt right until I became involved in

Native American spiritual ceremonies.

I love their ceremonies that honor Mother Earth, and their connection to their spiritual ancestors. While living in Idaho's ski resort, Ketchum, I discovered the book, Mother Earth Spirituality: Native Paths to Healing Ourselves and Our World, by Oglala Sioux lecturer and ceremonial leader Ed McGaa, Eagle Man. I contacted Eagle Man through his publisher and invited him to talk about his books at our local library. A few months later Eagle Man arrived in Idaho.

People were so impressed by his talk on the natural way of living they asked me to organize a sweat lodge ceremony and vision quest in late September with Eagle Man. Twenty-five people signed up for the ceremony, with others wanting to join. People had to be turned away because of the limited space inside the sweat lodge. First, Eagle Man showed us how to gather willow saplings for the sweat lodge and bend the twigs to create our lodge. People donated blankets and tarps, which others brought lava rocks for the pit. Three hours later, we had the materials for our first sweat lodge. By early evening our sweat lodge was built and we were ready to begin our ceremony, in a secluded place near Sun Valley ski resort.

People from California and Northern Idaho, as well as a Hopi medicine man from Arizona, were there to seek the natural way to spirituality. Eagle Man smudged each person with sage, and blessed them.

Inside the hot sweat lodge Eagle Man recited an ancient Lakota prayer and poured a ladle of water over the rocks, as a woman drummed softly. He blew the Eagle whistle to summon in the ancestor spirits. It felt as if the wings of an eagle flew past my face. Minutes later we were drenched in steam from the hot lava rocks. The drumming stopped, and Eagle Man recited another Lakota prayer and beseeched the Creator and Four Directions. He then asked the group to introduce themselves, and give what animal or object in nature they were closest to. Then we were asked to provide a prayer.

Ed McGaa "Eagle Man" and author in Ketchum, Idaho

I saw and felt the spirits that night. Later, others confided they had witnessed faces in the fire pit. Rainbows have been my totem since my vision in 1985. Eagle Man gave me the name 'Rainbow Woman', and my daughter, Camille, who gave the most eloquent prayer of all, (asking for the healing of all children and that all humanity learn to love one another and accept each other for their differences) was named 'White Wolf', or Tashuunka Manitou Sah, in Lakota.

After the ceremony several people talked openly about their personal experiences inside the sweat lodge. Some felt tingling in their bodies, a young woman watched an eagle spirit fly in, and an older woman believed she was healed from an illness, but didn't go into details. Five people decided to hike into the mountains to pray and meditate, to complete their Vision Quest, while I stayed behind with Eagle Man and several others and slept near the campfire, and Eagle Man slept in the sweat lodge to stay warm.

A Native American Vision Quest is a ceremony where a person spends one to four days and nights secluded in nature to find spiritual guidance and purpose, after fasting for two or three days. During this time of spiritual communication with the Creator and the Four Directions a person receives profound insight into themselves and the world. Many holy men have recounted visions of the future during a Vision Quest.

I prayed alone for a while, feeling the oneness of nature, grateful for Eagle Man's sacred sweat lodge ceremony and the special people who had attended the event. That night, as I slept under the stars, I dreamt of great Thunderbirds. The Thunderbird is a legendary creature of certain North American indigenous peoples. It is considered a supernatural bird of great power and strength. The Thunderbird has often been compared to the Phoenix, found in ancient cultures throughout the world.

Eagle Man taught us the importance of ceremony, and how ceremony can change the world. He talked of the weekend of August 16, 1987, when worldwide consciousness took place, in the form of a ceremony for peace and harmony that spread throughout the planet. Globally, humans gathered and beseeched their concept of a Higher Power for communicative peace to flourish across the continents, across the oceans, during The Harmonic Convergence.

L to R: Author's friend and author at Idaho pow wow

Dr. Jose Arguelles experienced a vision of The Harmonic Convergence in 1987, so he created a day determined by the Maya calendar. That ceremony spread around the world before the internet existed. Shortly after the global meditation weekend, the Berlin Wall came down, changing our world, seemingly overnight.

Eagle Man returned to Idaho several times, and became my mentor for the natural and indigenous way of life. That same year I met another great spiritual leader, Corbin Harney, of the Western Shoshone Nation, before his passing in 2007. I met Corbin during his visit to Boise, Idaho, where he conducted a special ceremony in the foothills. I had read his amazing book, The Way It Is: One Water…One Air…One Mother Earth, and I hoped to create a large gathering for peace at Sundance, Utah, owned by actor Robert Redford. I wrote to Robert Redford about my proposed conference and he replied with an interest, but later rescinded, due to the lack of space for such a large gathering of people. Corbin, an admirer of Robert Redford, was greatly disappointed that our conference in Sundance didn't happen. Corbin said, "We have to come back to the Native way of life. The Native way is to pray for everything. Our Mother Earth is very important. We can't just misuse her and think she's going to continue."

Corbin had protested against nuclear testing and uranium mining in Nevada during the 1990s. He had a powerful vision of the future. "A few years ago, I was praying to the water," Corbin said. "I was praying that it would run pure and clear, and that it would be able to take care of us for countless generations. The water came to me and spoke to me. It said: 'In a few years I'm going to look like water, but you're not going to be able to use me anymore.'"
Corbin's vision was right. Today we've seen how our oceans, rivers, and lakes have become contaminated with radiation, fertilizers, oil, gas and other toxins.

He said, "The old people used to say that the trees, the rocks, the birds, and the animals used to talk. They had a voice, and today, as I realize it, they still have a voice. My people always say that you have to take care of them in order for you to continue on. If you don't, when they die off, you are going to die off with them."

Corbin Harney, Spiritual Leader of the Western Shoshone Nation

Corbin wasn't a fatalist but realized that if humanity change and make a commitment to honor the Earth and all living creatures, our planet would die, and so would we. Corbin reminded us, "We, the people, are going to have to put our thoughts together to save our planet here. We have to start joining together to pray. We all have to try to keep our Mother Earth clean. We are going to have to join hands together the best way we can and do one thing: pray. We only have One Water…One Air…One Mother Earth."

I was honored to have known such a great man. When Corbin passed on July 10th, 2007, we lost a great spiritual leader who spoke his truth. Thankfully, we still have Ed McGaa, "Eagle Man," who continues to speak his own truth about the environment and returning to the old ways of honoring and respecting Mother Earth.

During those years I attended pow wows in Southern California, Oregon, Canada, and throughout Idaho, meeting wonderful American Indians and feeling a great kinship to them. There were also other wonderful Idaho sweat lodge ceremonies I attended through the years. Today, it's been years since I attended Native American ceremonies, but I still practice those ceremonies at home, burning sage or sweet grass, and praying each morning to the four directions, the animals, Mother Earth, Grandmother Moon, and Grandfather Sun, and all life.

Since childhood I have always sensed a powerful relationship with nature, how everything has consciousness, and how everything on planet Earth is fused with Creator's essence and spirit.

I don't want to be an old woman and tell my great grandchildren about the good old days, when we used to have pristine forests, great whales and dolphins, fresh water, and oceans abundant with life. I want to see Mother Earth flourish again, and I want future generations to see the beauty I've seen as a child—not a dying world. *Mitakuye Oyasin*—we are related to all things.

Chapter Twelve
S.O.S. from Spirit

In 2000 I moved to Tucson, Arizona. That fall I experienced one of the strangest dreams ever. I stood in a field staring at a giant apple tree. As I watched the tree, the leaves suddenly shriveled and died, and the apples dropped to the ground. Then it happened—the entire trees was pulled straight down into the ground and vanished. Gone! I couldn't imagine what symbol the tree represented, or why it had disappeared into the ground, until the tragic events of September 11, 2001, in the place known as "The Big Apple," New York City.

On September 11, 2001, nineteen militants, associated with the Islamic extremist group al-Qaeda, hijacked four airliners and carried out suicide attacks against targets in the United States. Two of the planes were flown into the towers of the World Trade Center in New York City; the third plane hit the Pentagon, just outside Washington, D.C.; and the fourth plane crashed in a field in Pennsylvania. Over 3,000 people perished during the attacks in New York City and Washington, D.C., including more than 400 police officers and firefighters.

Nagging questions remain unanswered about 9-11. Recalling my life-like dream from 2000, I know my dream had shown that more was involved than terrorists taking down the World Trade buildings. The tree didn't topple over; it went straight down into the ground, exactly like buildings taken down by an implosion with explosives. Buildings that are demolished this way ensure the building will fall into its own footprint, so nearby structures stay undamaged. To this day I intuitively sense that the citizens of the United States were lied to about the tragic events of 9-11. Someday the shocking truth will be uncovered.

I realize there are those who can't believe such a tragic event could have been perpetrated by those in the United States, but I can tell you that in the coming years new light will be shed on this heinous act that will anger and shock us. More than 1,400 engineers and architects have express significant criticism of the 9/11 Commission Report. Several even allege government complicity in the terrible acts of 9/11. You can Google this and find names of these courageous people who have stepped forward with the truth.

The World Trade Center, building 7, was 610 feet tall, 47 stories high, and although it was not hit by an airplane, it completely collapsed into a pile of rubble in less than 7 seconds at 5:20 p.m. on

9/11, seven hours after the collapses of the Twin Towers. However, no mention of this collapse appeared in the 9/11 Commission's "full and complete account of the circumstances surrounding the September 11, 2001 terrorist attacks."

During this time I felt an urgency to move back to Southern California. I didn't know why my spirit guides were sending an insistent message for me to move, but I listened. I felt it had to do with my sister Kathy. We hadn't talked in several years, after having a major argument. Was she was or Hector ill? Something was wrong, and I needed to contact her.

Whatever it was, spirit said it was urgent, so I acted on the feeling and moved back to Southern California. Meanwhile, I tried Kathy's last telephone number, and discovered her number had been disconnected. I wrote a letter and mailed it, hoping it would be forwarded to her new address. I also thought that if I told her that I had found our half-sister in Denton, Texas, she'd respond.

It was a miracle that I had found our half-sister Jean two months earlier, with the help of a researcher from Washington State. Jean had been born while Mom was in the Navy. Mom had fallen in love with a handsome naval officer named Hamilton, from Marin County, California, while stationed at Treasure Island, near San Francisco, in 1946. It was unclear if Hamilton had known about Mom's pregnancy at the time she left for Seattle's Florence Crittenton Home for Unwed Mothers, where Jean was born and relinquished for adoption at birth.

Because it was shameful during that time for an unwed mother to raise a baby alone, Mom's adoptive mother, Violet, pushed her into the adoption against her will. Mom later confided that it was the hardest thing she had ever done, because she was reliving her own childhood abandonment.

Finding Jean happened with the help from a human 'angel,' an adoption searcher in Seattle, who had seen my request for help on the internet. Within a short time, I had my half-sister's address and telephone number, and was able to contact her. My only regret was that Mom wasn't alive to meet her eldest daughter. I'm sure, though, she was responsible for the serendipitous events that lead me to Jean.

Kathy contacted Jean after receiving my letter, and then Jean called me to say that she had asked Kathy to reconcile with me. Not long after Jean's phone call, Kathy called and apologized for causing our lengthy falling-out. Once again, Kathy and I were friends and bonding as sisters, after many years of hurt and anger that so desperately needed to be healed.

One of my fondest memories is our drive to Mountain Spirit Center Buddhist Temple, a few miles outside of Tehachapi. Here we met Korean monk Mu Ryang Sunin, a tall man, with piercing blue eyes.

We were invited to join Mu Ryang Suin and two Korean women for a vegetarian lunch. Mu Ryang Sunin explained that he had studied engineering and also discovered the area was full of energy according to oriental principles of geomancy. The land had long been a place for Indians to conduct Vision Quests. Natural springs provided pure water, and electricity was harnessed by solar power and wind. The well water was reused for irrigation of native plants, a vegetable garden, and surrounding trees. He expressed that the monks had a deep concern for the surrounding environment.

On Sunday Kathy and I returned to the temple to participate in the Buddhist prayer ceremony. It was a spiritual day for us, which brought us back together as sisters.

When July arrived Jean flew in to Southern California to meet her sisters, and to spend a week with Kathy in Bear Valley.

We were amazed how our sister Jean resembled Mom in looks and gestures. This was the happiest I'd seen Kathy in years.

The events of 9-11 had plunged a great number of companies into a downward financial spiral, including Kathy's husband's business. Hector had lost several large government contracts for his aerospace parts business, forcing him to file bankruptcy. Soon Kathy and Hector's Bear Valley ranch-style home was foreclosed on. Kathy's life was falling apart and so was her health. She found it hard to swallow, an ailment that continued to get worse until a local doctor determined she had Polymyositis, a disease that affects the muscles in the upper part of the body.

The disease caused Kathy's muscles to atrophy, making it almost impossible for her swallow food. The steroid drug prednisone was prescribed, which gave Kathy some relief.

Articles on the disease stated that it was also linked to cancers, especially colon cancer, and I suspected there was more to her swallowing disease. Kathy also complained of feeling bloated all the time, and finally made another doctor's appointment. This time, several benign polyps were discovered and removed from her colon. That worried me. Did she have colon cancer? Did the stress of a personal and business bankruptcy, and losing their beautiful home and horses, affect her health? And what about the impact of Kathy's cigarette chain-smoking? My intuition said Kathy had undetected colon cancer.

During the years I was employed by a dentist, and that dentist claimed that he could tell when someone was experiencing major stress in their lives by the health of their teeth. If a person walked in with an abscess, the dentist asked if they some major event had taken place in their lives to upset them. The patient always said yes.

By Christmas Hector and Kathy had decided to retire to Argentina, where they could live comfortably on Hector's Social Security checks. Jean, my daughter Camille, and I questioned Kathy's hasty decision to leave Southern California for Buenos Aires, especially with her health problems. We tried to talk her out of it, but Kathy was determined to move.

In mid-March my husband Rick and I drove to Bear Valley to pick up some of my belongings, stored at Kathy's house since my move to Salt Lake City some months earlier. I found Kathy frail-looking. During our stay, I provided Kathy with Reiki treatments, which gave her a little energy, but the treatments weren't enough to alleviate her horrible pain. Before leaving I held my sister tightly, certain I'd never see her again, knowing this was our last time together. "Please don't cry, sis, I'll be fine," she said, averting her eyes from mine, so I couldn't see her true feelings. "I love you," she added.

"I love you, too, and I'll miss you," I said, overwhelmed with emotion and tears. She handed me a belated birthday card, which read:

Betsey, to a sister that I've missed and loved very much.

Here's to a wonderful celebration on your birthday. I hope all your dreams come true! All my love, Kathy.

Something in the card felt final. How I wanted to turn back time, and erase the angry years when we had been estranged. Such wasted time. At that moment I saw the pain in her eyes, and her profound sadness. Now I understood the urgency I had felt from spirit to return to Southern California. Spirit had warned me that Kathy needed me and was ill.

Visions of Kathy's untimely death had haunted me since childhood, when I had believed I could change her fate by making her walk backwards for a full day. Somehow, I had known we'd never grow old together.

Kathy and Hector flew to Buenos Aires at the end of March, despite our protests. Both Jean and I begged her to stay and live with one of us, but she wouldn't hear of it. When mid-April came, and Kathy hadn't called to let me know she was settled and all right, I panicked.

I contacted the U.S. Embassy in Buenos Aires and left urgent messages, believing they'd help me locate Kathy and Hector. They never returned any of my calls. There was nothing I could do except wait, and pray that Kathy or Hector would contact either me or Jean.

Kathy called Jean one week later, and apologized for not contacting us sooner. She said that Hector had been driving her back and forth from their home to a Buenos Aires clinic, an hour's drive away. Kathy's Polymyositis disease had made it impossible for her to eat; now she lived on only water and juice. And to add to her pain and sadness, her favorite Sheltie dog Prancer had vanished while a friend walked him in the Argentine countryside.

The next call I received from Kathy was devastating. Tests from Buenos Aires Medical Clinic confirmed Kathy had advanced cancer that had metastasized throughout her body—in her lungs, colon and brain. There was nothing they could do for her except give her mild pain medication and send her home. According to Kathy, Argentina had strict laws that banned the use of strong opiates (like morphine) for pain. It was unconscionable that a government would allow their terminally ill to endure pain without any strong medication.

During our conversation Kathy started to cry, but she regained her courage when I openly wept. "Please, sis, don't cry for me," she said, just above a whisper. Whenever Jean or I called Kathy our conversations were short, so we cherished the fleeting chats we had with her. We wanted to jump on a plane and bring her back to the United States, so she could get the care she so desperately needed now. Time, however, had run out - she had become too weak to travel. To add to our frustration, Hector didn't provide much information about Kathy's condition, due to his limited use of English. Jean and I believed that Kathy's doctor in California had missed malignant polyps in her colon, and because of her compromised immune system she had developed the Polymyositis. According to national statistics, colon cancer is the second-leading killer in the United States, after lung cancer.

July arrived, and early one morning I woke to hear Dad's voice call out my name, as if he stood beside my bed. There was nothing frightening about his voice, but I sensed he was there to guide Kathy to the Other Side. Immediately, I phoned Kathy about Dad's visit and assured her that Dad was near, and that she had nothing to fear. Kathy confirmed she felt a loving presence in the house, but couldn't identify it as Dad.

After our brief conversation, I wrote to Kathy:

Dear Sister,

I would give anything to keep you with us a little longer. Now I know why I moved to California from Tucson. That reason was you, and our need to reconcile our relationship. We became friends again and met our wonderful half-sister Jean.

I will never forget the day we spent at the Buddhist temple - just sisters bonding again. Thank you for those wonderful memories, which I will cherish always.

Dad is near, watching and protecting you. I know your spirit guides are there for you as well. Don't be afraid to call on them to take you to a place of love and peace.

Remember, love in an incredible force, the God force of existence that never ends. Always know you have touched so many lives with your humor, love and caring spirit. And if angels give out brownie points, you have certainly earned hundreds and hundreds of them.

I love and miss you so very much. We will always be together. Love, your sis, Betsey

Kathy was usually asleep when I called Argentina and if she happened to be awake, our conversations lasted less than three minutes. Then on July 15, I was stunned when Kathy answered the phone. She was lucid, and reported her pain had subsided. Although she had asked the nurse to cut back on the mild pain medication, Jean and I suspected that her increased energy meant she was in the final stages before death. Many terminally ill patients report this increase of energy and euphoria before their death.

The next call was from Hector on July 19, at 11 o'clock Mountain Time. Hector said Kathy had lapsed into a coma. Minutes later he phoned back to say Kathy passed, free at last from her pain. Suddenly it dawned on me why Kathy had died on July 19—our father's birthday. It was Dad's way of validating that he was there to guide Kathy over to the Other Side.

How strange it was that Kathy had taken Mom's ashes to Argentina when she and Hector had moved there. Now Kathy and Mom's cremated ashes remained in Argentina.

Unable to see my sister one more time was difficult and not having any real closure to her death—this grieved me greatly. I wanted to obtain my sister's and mom's cremated ashes so I could scatter them near Idaho's Redfish Lake, but Customs regulations forbade it.

Sometimes I forget that spirit is always listening. Months after Kathy passed, she returned to validate her love and existence on the Other Side. Through the years Kathy and I often talked about death, and what we'd find on other the Other Side; and how we are pure spirit and capable of manifesting anything, instantly, with our thoughts on the Other Side. I'd soon discover she had learned how to manifest reality in our physical world by focusing her thoughts on an object.

Chapter Thirteen
Kathy's Validations

My first validation from Kathy took place one morning while my husband Rick and I read the Sunday newspaper on our deck in Salt Lake City, Utah. Kathy's dragonfly wind chime was hanging on a small tree that had recently withered and died. Unexpectedly the chimes rang out, as if a strong wind had stirred, but there was no wind. I turned around and saw the tree swaying back and forth as if an invisible hand had shaken it.

There was no logical explanation for the event—no wind, no earthquake. I asked aloud, "Kathy, if that's you, please show me another sign."

Only a week later my request was answered. The same tree

shook and the chimes rang out, and a large black and white dragonfly landed on the tree, remaining there for fifteen minutes while I photographed it.

Kathy had collect dragonfly outdoor decorations, so I knew this was her way of validating she was still watching over me. Jean also received a validation from Kathy one morning, when a large dragonfly flew into her kitchen and landed on her coffee pot. It remained there for several minutes before flying away. Coffee had been Kathy's favorite beverage.

That night, Jean dreamt that Kathy said, "You wrote the script, now you must play it out," which she interpreted it to mean that we plan our life before we come into this world. We are actors on the stage of life.

Through the months I dreamt of funerals, sensing a family death soon. Then I received the sad news from Jean that her husband of thirty-five years had died of cancer. I called Jean, and related the following story, sensing she needed faith that life exists after death. This true story was told on a late night radio talk show:

The caller said that he had had recurring dreams during his childhood of silver water, where babies were laughing and playing. He said the dreams were so incredibly vivid he knew they were real. Years later he married and had a son. One day his five-year-old son came to him and said, "I'm so glad you and Mommy are my parents. My last parents were mean to me."

The man was perplexed, until his son added, "Do you remember, Daddy, when we played with the babies in the silver water, and you promised to be my daddy, and I promised to come back as your son?" The man was completely stunned by his son's strange revelation, because he had never revealed his childhood dream to anyone!

On July 9, 2013, in a dream, Kathy spoke to me and said she was throwing a surprise birthday party for me. I kept telling her it wasn't my birthday, but she insisted it was. Later that day, I discovered my granddaughter Candace had given birth to a baby boy, born five weeks premature. Kathy loved holidays and birthdays, and this was her announcement of my great grandson's birth. This was just the beginning of Kathy's visitations.

Again, Kathy validated her presence during the Thanksgiving holiday 2013. Our newly purchased stereo suddenly turned off by itself whenever we turned on the Kool Oldies FM radio station. The first time the radio turned off was during the song, Cathy's Clown, written and recorded by The Everly Brothers. Kathy was there to remind me of the times I sang Cathy's Clown to her during our teen years.

It was in December that I woke early to see a brilliant light flash through the hallway toward the kitchen. I sensed it was Kathy. There is no light source in our dark hallway to explain the flash of light. Even our cat, Comet, sensed her presence one night when his hair stood on end and he hissed in the hall at an unseen presence. There are countless stories of cats interacting with spirits that were invisible to the human eye. Animals of all kinds seem to possess a sixth sense that allows them to be more in tune with the invisible world, an ability that humans lost eons ago.

Recently I read the story of a cat that predicts the death of people at a nursing home when he jumps on their lap. Are cats telepathic, and able to see dead people? Absolutely!

At first, my husband and I believed the radio had an electrical problem, but the times the radio shut off usually happened on the weekend and at twenty-minute intervals, around seven in the morning or at night. Sometimes the radio shut off the moment I walked by it, or when we mentioned Kathy's name.

Not only did the kitchen stereo-radio turn off, but my husband's computer began shutting off by itself. Kathy even made a kitchen scrub brush levitate off the counter and into the sink.

We thought Kathy had made her last visit on December 29, 2013, but, later, we discovered our heavy binoculars placed in the middle of the floor in my husband's office.

Kathy obviously had an important message for us.

Other manifestations included Kathy's ability to switch on a night light in the kitchen.

Kathy vanished after the holidays, as if her mission was complete. What was her mission? It was to encourage me to write about my validations and experiences with the Other Side. At the time, I was starting a new book, *Earth Energy,* and never considered writing about my own experiences. Kathy's mission, I believe, was to have me to write this book, and she could move on—maybe. Kathy returned for another holiday on Easter, and turned off the radio again. She's also acknowledged her presence before several psychic readings I've given lately, by shutting off the radio.

One thing is for certain, Kathy hasn't lost her sense of humor on the Other Side and her sense of mischief. I imagine her looking down on me from her place there, with a glint of mischief in her eyes, and wearing a broad smile, knowing she pushed her sister into writing this book so that she could impart an important message to me and all who read it: don't wait until your loved ones pass over to tell them every day how much you love and appreciate them. Tell them now.

Life on Earth is too short, and we never know when we will die, or when a family member or friend will take their last breath. So celebrate life each moment, each day. Live each day as if it were your last. Be more loving, more thoughtful, and more appreciative. Sing more, dance more, compliment more, laugh more, cry more, and embrace more.

It's all about forgiveness, love, compassion, and acceptance. The love we share with family and friends is never lost; it only transmutes into another form of energy and into another dimensional existence. Love is endless, it lasts forever.

Betsey's sister, Kathy

Chapter Fourteen
Premonitions

Through the years my spirit guides have dropped by to tell me about homicides and missing person cases, which I'm not keen on pursuing. Sometimes, however, they are persistent. There are gifted psychics who work with law enforcement agencies to track down killers and missing persons, but as an empath, I knew I'd feel too much of the victim's pain to embark on this type of psychic work.

My friend, Ann Druffel, renowned author and earth mysteries investigator, worked with the late psychic medium Armand Marcotte in Los Angeles. I met Armand briefly while temporarily employed at Stephan Schwartz's Los Angeles Mobius Group during the early 1980s. Stephan's Mobius Group employed gifted psychics to remote view homicides and missing persons' cases, and even for archaeology.

One day a request came in to the Mobius Group to locate the whereabouts of two men who had vanished in a remote part of Canada while hunting. Two of the psychics believed the men were still alive, but my mom and I discussed the case and we both felt that the men had died from hypothermia in the extreme cold. Days later our intuition proved sadly correct; the men had died from hypothermia.

I met Ann for the first time at the Mobius Group, and one year later she conducted regressive hypnosis on my mom and me, regarding that weird roar my parents and I experienced on the lonely highway in Northern Idaho when I was eight-months-old, and how my parents lost two hours of time they couldn't account for. The

Ann had co-authored several books with renowned psychic/medium Armand Marcotte, including The Psychic and the Detective, an account of comprehensive cases which Marcotte worked on at the request of various police and sheriff departments in Los Angeles, Riverside, San Diego, San Bernardino, Imperial counties of California, the Southwest and the Midwest.
Marcotte had an uncanny ability to provide clues to unsolved cases, such as the vicious murder of renowned parapsychologist and author D. Scott Rogo. He had also co-authored the well-known book, *The Tujunga Canyon Contacts* (1980) with Ann Druffel, about alien abductions taking place in Southern California.

Marcotte was given credit by the Los Angeles Police Department (LAPD) for his part in solving Rogo's murder. Ann and

Marcotte's book, *The Psychic and the Detective,* was intended as a working manual for law enforcement officials who wanted to consult qualified psychics in solving difficult crimes.

As for me, I never know when spirit will provide information about a missing person's case. In one particular Idaho missing person's case, I visualized how the missing woman vanished near a reservoir. Police, tracking dogs and people on foot searched for the missing woman for days near the Boise's reservoir and couldn't find her. In my vision, I was shown the woman in her car, having a heated argument with a man. The man jumped out of the car and the woman hit the gas pedal and plunged over an embankment and into the reservoir, where she drowned. I didn't go to law enforcement agencies, believing they'd probably think I was crazy or perhaps involved in the case. So I waited, sensing they'd make the discovery and they did!

Law enforcement agencies have been known to suspect psychics in a missing person's case or murder case after they stepped forward with unknown details related to a case. Months later, when the water in the reservoir receded enough to make the grisly find, the woman's car was discovered with her body in the driver's seat. News reports stated that murder was suspected in the case.

Another case that haunted me for days was the case of an adorable eight-year-old boy who vanished, according to the mother and her boyfriend. Law enforcement and members of the public combed the area, and police dogs were used to pick up the child's scent. Days went by without any clues to the child's whereabouts.

The first time I watched the news report, I felt he'd been

murdered. In my mind I watched, as he stood beside water, smiling and waving goodbye, free at last from the abuse he'd endured for years from his mother and her boyfriend. People rallied around the distraught couple, and all the while I knew they were involved with the boy's disappearance and death. Their grief was an act.

Days later the boy's body was discovered in a canal. There were signs of physical abuse. It was heartbreaking. Then the mother and boyfriend confessed to the murder, and were arrested on murder charges. People who had supported the couple from the beginning were shocked and angered.

I've foreseen many of these missing cases, and I'm not always sure I'm right. Again, I must say that these missing person's cases are just too disturbing for me to view as an empath, and I block the visions whenever I can.

Chapter Fifteen
Client Readings

The names of the people mentioned in this chapter have been changed to protect their identity and privacy. It is with great love and appreciation I include a few psychic readings I've provided for clients through the years.

First, I meditate, asking my spirit guides and my client's guides to come through. Next, I prepare a personalized astrological chart, usually 10-12 pages long, taken from three esoteric sources. Each chart takes approximately two days to put together. I also use Medicine Cards and numerology which helps me tune into my client's energy field.

On the day of the reading, I begin each reading by saying, "We were all given the divine gift of Free Will. If you believe that you have no control over your life because of destiny or that you brought in so-called bad karma, you will never rise to your highest spiritual potential. You are the creator and the master of your life! So what I tell you today is your probable future, but remember, there are many probable roads to take in life. Which one will you choose?"

Zahara's Story
Zahara said she found my website by accident, and felt drawn to contact me after reading my posts and information. I always know the right people are sent to me for readings.

Zahara was born in the Mideast in 1983, and that's all I knew from her birth information, until I prepared her astrological chart. I was shocked to see how her planets and their placement in the astrological houses represented her past lives in healing and medicine. She was also blessed with amazing psychic/medium abilities. Everything from spirit and her chart indicated she was in a health-related occupation, but that she needed to acknowledge her psychic gifts.

On the morning of the reading, the first thing I said to Zahara was, "You have amazing psychic abilities and should be the one giving me a psychic readings."

She laughed, and said, "You're right about my psychic abilities. In fact you are so right about everything in my astrology chart. I knew that you were the right psychic for me."

"Does your work involve healthcare?" I asked.

She acknowledged that her work involved the health-related field. I sensed she had a past life as a nurse as I continued, "You are going through some huge changes and you were recently separated from a boyfriend or husband, and need to move."

Again she was shocked by my accuracy, and said her life had been in turmoil.

"I see you moving soon, but don't know where to go. Have you sensed someone helping you, like an older female that passed on?"

"That's my grandmother. I feel her around me all the time," she said.

"I feel that you see spirits all the time, and you had a rough time as a child because people didn't understand you."

There was a long silence, and then Zahara began to sob the phone.

I was perplexed. "I'm so sorry I upset you, but why are you crying?" I questioned. My heart went out to her, feeling her pain, since I had experienced the same ridicule and shame as a child. Zahara continued. "As a child no one believed me when I described my spirit visitations. People and children used to laugh at me in my country. This is the first time anyone has acknowledged my gift."

Zahara was an Indigo, one of the special new children born on this planet to raise the vibrational rate with their special God-given talents in the metaphysical studies, music, art, science, and math. I told her about her mission, and why she had chosen to come into the world at this time, and how important it was for her to use her gifts.

Earlier that day Kathy had made it known she would be stopping by for the reading, when she turned off the radio that morning. I began by drawing seven Medicine Cards. The first card was the armadillo, a small creature with a hard shell covering its body. It told me that Zahara feared her psychic powers, and had hidden them for years. Next, Kathy guided me to the Spirit card, which said Zahara was constantly seeing spirits. And then I pulled the Butterfly card, which indicated Zahara was going to transform from an egg, to a caterpillar and then a beautiful butterfly. This year would bring extraordinary changes for her.

Zahara, I was told, would one day become famous as a writer, but she still needed to tap into her inner talents and believe in herself. In a vision she appeared to be signing autographs for a book that she would write about her own metaphysical experiences, which would help those who have been ridiculed all their lives because of their psychic abilities.

Zahara confirmed everything that I had given her in the reading, and she was once again joyful about her life and the positive changes coming for her in the months and years ahead. It was an honor to read for such a gifted Indigo.

Claire's Story

Claire, from Stockholm, Sweden, found me through a friend's referral. She was in her early thirties, and seemed very shy and unsure of herself. Through my spirit guides and her astrological chart I knew Claire had the ability to heal people and had not incorporated this gift into her life, although she felt it was her calling.

Claire told me all the things that prevented her from accomplishing her goals in life, and then I said, "Claire, what is really stopping you?"

There was a long silence, and then she answered as if a light bulb turned on. "Me!"

"That's right...you. You can do anything in life, and you brought these beautiful gifts into this life and have failed to us them because you're afraid to be your glorious self."

A month later Claire emailed me to say that she was pursuing her lifelong dream of holistic healing.

Jessica's Story

When Jessica met with me for a reading, immediately her departed father stepped forward to say that her mother was ill and wanted to pass and join Jessica's father on the Other Side. What I was told by Jessica's father was that her mother was making herself ill, and that if she continued with her depression she wouldn't be in the world much longer. He kept saying it wasn't her time to join him. Her mother had so much more living to do, and I asked Jessica to convey that to her mother.

Jessica was blown-away by my insight into her mother's current situation. Her father expressed how sorry he was for his anger and temper through the years, and for putting up a wall between them as father and daughter. This estrangement had caused Jessica to distrust men, which had created problem in her relationships. None of her relationships lasted. Jessica said the reading was healing, and she was anxious to relay the message to her mother from her departed father.

A follow-up email from Jessica said her mother was improving, and Jessica was in a new relationship.

Al's Story

Sometimes spirit is downright demanding, and it happened during Al's reading. Al, as I suspected, didn't make the appointment—his wife did, and right away I got the impression he had a giant wall around him. He didn't want to believe a thing I was going to tell him. Yikes!

Everything in his astrological chart said he was a famous artist of some kind, so I began by telling him that his astrological chart revealed fame. Then I revealed a message from his father. "Your father is stepping forward, and he wants you to get back into painting. He also apologizes for the things that were said."

Al confirmed that he was a recognized artist, and that he had a tough relationship with his father. Then I asked, "Why do I see you painting what looks like Native American Medicine Wheels and orbs everywhere? What connection do you have to these things?"

Al replied, "I see orbs all the time, and paint them. Orbs are in most of my paintings as are medicine wheels."

I was floored. Then I asked, "I sense you have strange experiences with celestial beings. Why am I getting this?"

Al was quiet and didn't answer, but his wife jumped in. "Oh my God, you are so right. When we had our log home in the Northwest, he began getting urgent messages from evolved beings."

"Al is supposed to write about their messages. Why isn't he doing it?" I asked.

Again his wife answered. "He feels it isn't time to write this book. He'll know when the time is right."

Al then asked about his health. "I keep hearing cancer, but I know you don't have it. Why do you think you have cancer?" I questioned, sensing he had cancer concerns.

Al admitted his greatest fear was cancer, and he was concerned about his recent cancer tests.

Understand, I never give negative readings, but when I keep hearing a word over and over in my head I know spirit wants me to talk about it. Before ending the session I said, "Al, know that you are fine and you don't have cancer. I guarantee it. You have much to do in life and there is a book out there that has your name on it. Spirit wants you to write it soon and include your amazing experiences with other worldly beings and the orbs."

Al's wife contacted me the next week to say Al's tests all came back negative. He was cancer free!

Kristina's Story

Kristina was hesitant to have a reading at first. She was becoming famous as a spiritual leader throughout the world and in great demand as a speaker on spiritual truth. After studying her astrological chart, I noticed that she had been a man in another lifetime, and a powerful Egyptian priest, and had misused her gift. In order for her to evolve, and remove negative issues from her past life, she had to be a truthful spiritual leader.

She understood and agreed.

Sadly, Kristina had had a miserable childhood, but through those events she had grown. The placement of Gemini throughout her chart gave her charisma and the ability to be a powerful speaker. Her sun air sign bestowed love and honors on her, and her two water signs gave her great intuition. She was given healing ability, charisma, and everything needed to make her a great spiritual leader, so long as she didn't misuse her God-given talents.

I cautioned her not to fall into the money trap, where fame and fortune would rule her life, or she'd lose her gifts and her fame. Since the reading Kristina has grown in fame, and become a beloved spiritual leader. Hopefully, she listened to what spirit conveyed to her and will apply those messages in her daily life.

Barbara's Story

Barbara was excited to get a reading, but there was something in her email that troubled me. She believed there was negative energy in her life, and during the reading she said a psychic had told her that she had occult powers and was Illuminati.

I couldn't contain myself when she gave me that information over the phone, and laughed aloud, not out of disrespect, but because her belief she possessed dark occult powers. Barbara was a Northwest mother of two, with a wonderful husband, yet she was convinced by a psychic she had been exposed to the Illuminati while attending college in England.

Everything from spirit and the information in her astrological chart indicated she was of the light, and had the potential to help others in their quest for spiritual truth. The more I tried to convince her that her last psychic's claim was completely wrong, the angrier she became. I was totally perplexed by her reaction. She soon revealed that she had gone to psychic after psychic, and if the psychic didn't confirm she was Illuminati, she moved onto the next psychic for confirmation.

After this reading I was completely drained of energy. Barbara's negativity had zapped my energy and probably her own with all her false beliefs. There was nothing more I could do but pray for her awakening to the light and the wonderful, positive gifts she was born with. How sad to waste such energy on the darkness she believed she had been given when in fact, she held so much light.

Debbie's Story

This is one of my stranger and sadder stories from my psychic readings. Debbie lived in Northern California with her family, and admitted that she was in some kind of serious trouble. I kept asking her spirit guides what kind of trouble—was it with the law, drugs, etc., but her guides indicated it wasn't any of the above. She was not willing to open up to me, but finally after some urging she claimed her home was haunted by evil spirits and poltergeist activity, which I had already sensed in meditation.

My next question to Debbie was, "Do you have a young son around twelve-years-old?"

"Yes, but why?" she asked.

"You and your son don't get along well do you?"

She reluctantly replied yes.

"Your attitude has upset your son greatly, and he's producing the poltergeist activity in your house. You and your son have many lessons to learn in this lifetime about healing and forgiveness."

Like Barbara, Debbie wanted to believe there were evil spirits residing in her house that were out to get her, but in reality she had activated her son's psychic ability through her negativity toward him. Debbie has aspirations and wanted to be a writer, although she didn't have the education to pursue her dream. I could see she could have this gift if she really wanted to change her life, but everything she said was negative and hopeless.

As our conversation went on for days by email, I could tell Debbie didn't want to get help or change. She stubbornly wanted to stay in her self-made rut. She wanted to believe that evil spirits controlled her life when she was the source of the problem, creating pessimism and transferring that negativity to her son.

My prayers are sent daily to Debbie that she has an epiphany and begins the healing process for her and her family.

My Frustration

My greatest frustration is in teaching people that we control our lives. The stars only guide us, and fate does not control our lives. We have beautiful free will to do anything we set our minds to—nothing is impossible. It may take time to achieve your dreams, but if you hold on steadfastly to those dreams, you'll achieve them.

Successful people in all walks of life have been discouraged in their lives, and told not to pursue their dreams, but they didn't listen. Instead, they fought on to become the people they are today; successful people in our world. It took hard work, determination and persistence, but they didn't give up. No matter what your dream may be, never give up! Visualize your dream in detail, and make it reality. Think outside the box, get out of your comfort zone, and be the best you can be by honoring your God-given talents.

The lesson we all must learn while we exist in our physical bodies is that like the Other Side, we create our reality, our physical world, through our thoughts. The only difference is that thoughts become instant reality on the Other Side, but for us earthlings it takes a little longer to manifest our hopes, dreams and wishes.

Chapter Sixteen
Answers from Spirit

Over the course of my life I've had spirit warnings about deaths, as well as personal and global warnings. No doubt, I owe my life to my spirit guides and their patience with me. They've saved my life from car accidents, choking, suffocating in a snow bank, drowning, an airplane crash, near-fatal asthma attacks, and a pine tree falling on me while camping. There were also other near death incidents as well; like nearly falling from a mountain ledge, and hemorrhaging from a benign tumor.

Obviously my spirit friends have kept me around for a while longer to help others on their spiritual journey, and I'm grateful for their love and continued guidance, as I write my books and provide psychic readings for my beautiful clientele.

Through visions, my intuition, and my personal experiences and dreams, I've been given some answers to what lies beyond the veiled curtain we call Death. Believe me, I don't have all the answers to life's infinitesimal mysteries, but I have a real sense of what lies beyond. So I offer my insights from my spirit guides, Peekaboo and Patoy, and pray this information will help you when a loved one passes on to the Other Side. After helping a great many people, including myself, deal with grief, I'm still amazed by the constant validations from Spirit.

The questions included here have been asked by family, friends and clientele.

Question: What happens when we first cross over to the Other Side?
Answer: It all depends on our individual belief systems. When we pass over we become pure energy thought forms, and we create any scene that suits us. However, a large number of souls believe a heaven exists for the righteous and a hell exists for evil people. For those who believe this, depending on the type of person they have deemed themselves to be, they will see either a heaven or a hell. Our guides are always there to help us get reacquainted with our new surroundings again and how to us our mental powers again to create our environment.

For others who have had a long illness or died violently or tragically, they may sleep for a while, which can be months or years in Earth time. Sometimes the soul doesn't realize it has died, and spirit guides rush to their aid. Unfortunately, there are people who have died angry or full of hate, and haunt houses and buildings, using their energy in negative ways. They get trapped in a state of limbo and can't get free. The ethereal space around our planet is full of trapped, confused and angry souls and those souls need help to move on to continue on their spiritual evolution.

Question: Does everyone have a spirit guide?

Answer: Spirit guides are incorporeal beings who are assigned to you before you reincarnate into a physical body. They help nudge and guide you through life. Sometimes guides will stay through your entire life, and sometimes others replace them to help with specific life lessons. They may appear as male or female energy, but in reality they are pure energy. You are never alone. Usually guides are souls who have had physical incarnations. At times, a spirit guide will take on the appearance of a loved one who has died, to make the transition easier for the newly deceased person. From time to time more evolved beings and angels step in to help us fulfill our earthly mission.

Question: Is there a difference between spirit guides and angels?

Answer: Guardian angels are highly evolved beings or energy intelligence and have never existed in a physical body since their inception. They can be called upon for any reason and have direct access to the Akashic records, the universal computer. Spirit guides assist us through life and provide insight, inspiration, and a helping hand when needed. Spirit guides are learning too, and haven't evolved as far as angels.

Question: Are we judged by God on the Other Side?

Answer: No. God, or Creator, does not judge souls. You judge yourself for the positive and negative things you've done in the span of your life. Many people who have NDEs (near-death experiences) tell that they had a life review, like a movie, of everything done in a lifetime. You experience it all. This can be quite painful, but it serves to help the soul evolve and prepare for the next incarnation.

Question: So if there isn't a heaven or hell, what do souls do on the Other Side?

Answer: Excellent question. Like I answered before, we create our heaven or hell. A good analogy of the Other Side is the 1998 movie, *What Dreams May Come,* starring Robin Williams, Cuba Gooding, Jr., and Annabella Sciorra.

In the story Chris Nielsen (Robin Williams) has an idyllic life with artist Annie Collins (Annabella Sciorra) and their two children. Then one day a car accident takes the life of their two beautiful children, Ian and Marie. Life becomes difficult - Annie suffers a mental breakdown and the couple contemplates divorce.

Finally they decide to reconcile, but Chris is killed in a car crash. After his death he remains earthbound and tries to communicate with Annie to help her cope with her horrible losses. When his attempts don't help Annie's deep sorrow, he moves on.

Chris awakens in Heaven and learns that what he sees there is from his own imagination. He's created his own heaven. Soon Chris meets his spiritual guide, Albert (Cuba Gooding, Jr.). Albert guides Chris in this new afterlife. He also teaches Chris about his existence in heaven, and how to shape his little corner, and to travel to others' "dreams." Meanwhile, Annie commits suicide after years of depression. She finds herself in a hellish place until Chris, in his endless love for Annie, shows her how to join him in his heaven.

Chris and Annie are reunited with their children in their heaven. At the end Chris proposes they reincarnate so he and Annie can experience life together again. The film ends with Chris and Annie meeting again as young children in a situation that parallels their first meeting.

To get back to the original question, souls can do anything on the Other Side, such as explore new worlds and the stars, watch over loved ones on Earth, and take classes on any subject: the arts, music, writing, math, science, etc. Souls have a universe of options.

Question: I read somewhere that a soul can reincarnate every 18 minutes. Is this true, and how does the soul find the right parents? What if they have reincarnated already?

Answer: There are currently over seven billion human souls on Earth, and I'm sure they are returning faster than every 18 minutes. It is estimated that 134 million babies are born per year. How soon a soul reincarnates it entirely up to them. There is always a choice, but some souls are very impatient and decided to reincarnate immediately after death. There are countless stories of souls who reincarnated soon after death, especially in third world countries like Tibet and India. This is usually a bad idea because the soul needs more time to evaluate its previous life before taking on a new earthly body. From what I've learned, most souls reincarnate within one hundred years, which gives them time to access their Akashic soul records. Spirit guides are there to assist the newly arrived soul plan for the next adventure.

As far as finding the right parents, that's a mutual agreement between you and your soul friends. Your mother might decide to return as your sister in the next incarnation, or your father might be an uncle, or your brother might become your child. Most souls like to stay together and work on spiritual lessons together. There are some souls who want to seek new relationships, and that's perfectly fine too.

Not all growth happens in one lifetime, or in this earthy plane; it can be done on the Other Side without a physical body. But soul growth is so much faster in the physical realm, and the tests and lessons much harder. Reincarnation is real, and allows the soul to manifest itself again in this physical world, or in other worlds, in order to evolve.

Question: Hollywood actress Shirley MacLaine suggested in her new book, *What If,* that six million Jews and millions of others systematically murdered in Hitler's death camps in World War II were balancing their karma for crimes committed in past lives and that cosmologist Professor Stephen Hawking may have subconsciously given himself his debilitating motor neurone disease of ALS. How do you feel about this?

Answer: Shirley has always had a way of pushing buttons with her metaphysical, new age beliefs. I totally disagree with her when it comes to karma. Souls can take on great hardships, disasters, and disabilities to evolve much faster as spiritual beings. It is their choice. In some cases when a person murders another, the victim and the murderer have a specific karmic tie with each other from a past life. If a murder is committed, there is always karma, either instant or in another lifetime. There is no escaping the cosmic *Law of Cause and Effect*. Other times there is no karmic link, but each soul must work out their individual karma from past lives. Stephen Hawking may have decided that experiencing such a debilitating disease would help him advance on the spiritual ladder, and I'd say it has worked. He has overcome great obstacles and helped many people with ALS who would have given up without someone like Hawking to inspire them.

Karma is growth and evolution.

Question: What happens to babies and infants when they die?

Answer: These souls have chosen to leave early as a soul lesson. Sometimes the lesson involved the parents, and sometimes the infant's soul. There are no accidents in life, only lessons. Once the infant has crossed over, there are loving spirit guides to assist them until they become spiritually mature again. Some psychic believe that these are souls that committed suicide in a past life and return to make up this time to satisfy the karmic debt of suicide. I don't think this is always the case. Each soul decides what lessons they want to learn in this lifetime. Sometimes the soul realizes that the picked the wrong parents, and can't achieve certain positive experiences and soul lessons.

You say life is unfair when a baby dies, but you are wrong. Life is wonderfully fair and just. When an infant or young baby dies we cry and grieve for them, but the child does not need to be here anymore. They have already advanced, like skipping a grade in school. When a person is sick and dying, their faith is tested. How will they react and do the things needed for further spiritual advancement? Life is a never-ending school, a classroom of countless lessons.

Question: Suppose I had an argument with my mother or father before they died. Will they carry their anger to the Other Side?

Answer: Never will a good person who has passed hold anger in their heart for petty arguments and disagreements. Death doesn't change a person's character or personality. However, there are souls who have carried deep resentment and hate in their hearts because of injustices and untimely deaths, which keeps them earthbound and reliving the past. These malevolent ghosts haunt houses and produce a lot of negative energy at those who enter their world. Until these sad souls learn to release their hate and anger they will be trapped in an endless limbo world. Only love and forgiveness will release them from their eternal hell.

Questions: Can you tell me more about ghosts?

Answer: Most often a soul doesn't realize they have died and keep repeating the events that lead to their death, a kind of loop in space. Sometimes they didn't believe in anything beyond the physical world, and are trapped in their own limbo world. Prayers can help them to get back into the flow of everlasting life again. Unfortunately, there are souls who refuse to enter the light and evolve, and it might take hundreds, and maybe even thousands of Earth years for them to realize their mistake.

There are some souls that are trapped on the Earth plane by a negative force or forces that prevent them from moving forward into the higher spiritual realm. A positive mind propels us forward, and negative ones set us back. As I stated earlier, these sick minds can be healed by those in the spiritual realm or by human prayers.

Question: How long does it take for my deceased loved one to contact me?

Answer: Time, as we know it here on Earth, doesn't exist to them. Our loved ones hear our thoughts and prayers, which pull them to us instantly. They are around us all the time. Often their signs and messages are dismissed because most people don't want to believe that spirits can communicate with us from the spirit world. It may take years before you are aware or open to their validations. Sometimes it happens within moments of their passing, or it may take hours, days or even years. There are no set rules.

There are well-known mediums that make it seem like spirits can be summoned on demand, but this is not true! It seems more likely that the medium is reading someone's thoughts about their deceased loved one than actually getting spirit information.

I'm sure your next question is how do I know if I've received validation of their existence on the Other Side? Well, it's those things you call coincidences, but they aren't coincidences. Do you hear their favorite song played whenever you turn on the radio? Do you hear your name whispered before you wake up in the morning? Do you smell their favorite scent or perfume? Did you have a vivid dream where they spoke to you, and that dream seemed real? Did you feel someone stroking your face with a feather-like touch? Doe butterflies or dragonflies hover over you? Did a seeming miracle take place in your life, and you can't explain how it happened? Did an inspiration pop into your head out-of-the-blue one morning or did you receive a warning that saved your life?

Did you know that countless songwriters, authors, and

inventors, claim their invention, song or inspiration came to them in a dream or a sudden inspiration?

These are all validations from spirit of their eternal love and guidance.

Question: Why do groups of people chose to die together?

Answer: All through time groups of people have exited the planet in large numbers and this is a conscious decision for all involved. Those who leave the planet in a large group, by plane crash, boating accident, natural or non-natural disaster, choose to do so for great advancement of the soul. These groups usually reincarnate together—decisions that were made on the Other Side. Those who have died trying to save others by their heroic deeds and compassion during a disaster or great tragedy will evolve the soul quickly

Question: What happens to those who commit suicide?

Answer: Some believe suicide means eternal hell and no redemption, but they are completely wrong. Suicides do not have any particular punishment, except for the soul's choosing. However, any problems that were not faced in this life will be faced in another. There are different reasons for suicide—such as those with terminal diseases and in extreme pain, depression, mental illness, and those running from their problems, which is the hardest lesson for that soul. Escaping life's problems and taking your life is wrong and a type of suicide that the soul may spend many lifetimes resolving.

If a person kills himself believing that the act will destroy his consciousness forever, then this false idea may severely impede his soul's progress and be intensified by guilt.

Remember the soul judges self, so it is the soul's duty to

either find forgiveness in self or torture self in their own created hell. As I said before, Creator, or God, does not judge us, never has and never will. Those who commit suicide to stop endless pain from a terminal illness, or accidentally die from a drug overdose, will find forgiveness faster on the Other Side than those who run from their problems and commit this act. Prayers of love and forgiveness are always needed for these souls.

In Jane Robert's channeled book, *The Seth Material*, Jane was told by the entity Seth that after a suicide teachers are available to explain the true situation. Various therapies are used. For example, the personality may be led back to the events prior to the decision. Then the personality is allowed to change the decision. An amnesia effect is induced, so that the suicide itself is forgotten. Only later is the individual informed of the act, when he is better able to face it and understand it. Sometimes the personality refuses to accept the face of death. The individual knows quite well that he is dead in your terms, but he refuses to complete the psychic separation. Now: There are instances of course where the individuals concerned do not realize the fact of death. It is not a matter of refusing to accept it, but a lack of perception. In this state such an individual will also be obsessed with earthly concerns, and wander perhaps bewildered throughout his home or surroundings.

Unfortunately, there are a huge number of souls trapped in this reality, and someday when humans have learned how to clear the ethereal band surrounding Earth, these lost souls will someday be released from their self-imposed prison.

Seth continued: Those who understand thoroughly that

reality is self-created will have the least difficulty [on the Other Side]. Those who have learned to understand and operate in the mechanics of the dream state will have great advantage. A belief in demons is highly disadvantageous after death, as it is during physical existence. A systematized theology of opposites is also detrimental. If you believe, for example, that all good must be balanced by evil, then you bind yourself into a system of reality that is highly limiting, and that contains within it the seed of great torment.

Actor Robin Williams committed suicide inside his home by strangulation on August 11, 2014. He had suffered for years from depression, and substance abuse. It was revealed that he was diagnosed with Parkinson's disease, a degenerative disorder of the central nervous system, which might have contributed to his suicidal thoughts.

Shortly after Robin William's death, it was reported that he began turning on the television to watch his favorite comedy shows in the house where he died. Watchmen at the California mansion are convinced his ghost is lurking there. A neighbor said: "Security goes in every couple of hours to check the alarm system but several times now the TV has been on when they've arrived."

The source said that once a stand-up show was playing starring the late Richard Pryor, who was a pal before his death in 2005. "It's typical Robin—to be playing practical jokes and making people laugh, even in the afterlife"

Even in death, Robin's spirit is still the same. My sense is that Robin wanted the world know he still has his sense of humor and he's doing just fine on the Other Side.

Question: What is your favorite book on reincarnation?

Answer: Actually I have two favorite books. I love Brian Weiss's books, but my favorite book was his first, *Many Lives, Many Masters,* and another favorite for me is *The Search for Om Sety* by Jonathan Cott. *The Search for Om Sety* is probably one of the most convincing and powerful books on reincarnation. Born in England, Dorothy Eady was pronounced dead after a fall as a child, but mysteriously came back to life. Shortly after the fall she changed and began to talk about Egypt, a place she'd never visited. For the next sixty-five years, Dorothy, later known as Omm Sety, worked and lived in Cairo, Egypt, a place she called "home." She stunned archaeologists with her intimate knowledge of ancient Egyptian daily life and the religious rituals of the people. She was instrumental in the discovery of unknown archaeological sites at the time, recalling her life in ancient Egypt where she lived in the court of Pharaoh Sety the First as his secret lover. During that time Omm Sety had committed suicide because she had become pregnant by His Majesty, as she referred to him, an act was punishable by death. In order to prevent shame for His Majesty, Pharaoh Sety, she committed suicide. He then searched through time and space, over thousands of years, to find her in Egypt as the reincarnation of Dorothy Eady. He appeared to her daily in Egypt, professing his undying love for her. The information Dorothy provided archaeologists through the years could not have been known by Dorothy. This is an extraordinary story—one of reincarnation and undying love that spanned thousands of years.

Question: It seems there is more homosexuality in the world than ever before? Does God condemn this act?

Answer: I will say this to you again—God never judges us and has created all souls equally. Actually, the soul is neither male nor female, nor any color. It is sad that people hold up the Bible and say it says this or that, but these are not God's words, they are man's words.

Remember Matthew 7:1, "Judge not least ye be judged." What it means that we will be judged when we judge others—this is the way of karma.

These souls might have incarnated too quickly and that past life as a male or female still is fresh in their subconscious. A great number of homosexuals are coming into the planet with a message for all of humanity—that the human soul is neither male nor female. It is a big lesson for all at this time to accept each other, and look beyond race, religion, and sexual preference.

We are all God's children and have a right to be here to learn lessons of love. When we despise someone we despise God, because we are made from his mind.

In the beautiful book, *Kiss of God: The Wisdom of A Silent Child*, Marshall Stewart Ball, a brilliant child who was born with severe disabilities and unable to speak or walk, stunned his parents with his ability to understand life and the concept of God. Since the age of six he had completed hundreds of pages of writings. Marshall wrote in 1994, at age seven, "To judge another is to Judge God."

Although Marshall was never told about reincarnation, at age eight, he wrote, "Marshall has been here for millions of lifetimes."

Marshall is one of the new children, here to reteach us the art of love, compassion and understanding. As Marshall wrote, "Perfect love kindly will give each thought special direction," and "Answers come to good listeners that hear God. Go to God and God will teach you."

Creator's love is so great for all souls, it's all encompassing. Everyone is beautiful in God's eyes.

Why do humans hate others because of their skin color, their religion, and their sexual preference? In the spiritual realm none of this exists, and there is no reason to hate, yet on the earthly plane we find endless reasons to hate each other. It's senseless.

It's time we see the divine light in all God's creations.

Question: I've heard the expression "new souls." Can you elaborate on what this means?

Answer: God created all souls at the same time, but some souls have gone through the physical reincarnation progress much longer than others. Some souls have decided to visit this earthly plane for the first time and may have a hard time adjusting to the new experience. Some souls never need to go through this process of reincarnation for further evolution.

Question: There are stories of extraterrestrials seen with departed relatives. Do they access this reality?

Answer: Excellent question and a hard one to answer. From what I've sensed there are endless dimensions and worlds that co-exist with Earth. Parallel dimensions are being explored by scientists in the world of quantum physics.

Is it true that the Other Side could be accessed by a variety of beings? I believed it is possible. Everything is vibration, and there are many beings who are highly evolved, both spiritually and intellectually, that can move through time portals and space. I've always felt we are watched all the time by unseen beings, and everything we do and say is known and recorded.

Theoretical scientists believe time as we know it does not exist. The past, present and future are all happening at once, but on different planes of existence. Many times we get glimpses of a probable future with a vision or premonition, but that probable future can be changed. Does time travel exist? I have no doubt, and that many of the beings visiting us are from other time lines and dimensions.

We are just babies beginning to learn what the universe is made of and all its remarkable mysteries.

Question: Explain what you mean by "The Knowing."

Answer: It's a feeling that overcomes me and I know that I'm right about something or someone. I'll give you two examples of it. My husband and I were at a casino in Reno, Nevada. As we sat at a bar next to some slot machines, an overwhelming feeling told me to play the slot machines nearest us. Finally I got up a put a quarter in it and it paid $100.

Another example of "The Knowing": a friend was visiting and wanted a glass of red wine. We sat on a light sage-green sofa as I envisioned her dog or mine would knock over the wine glass. It would shatter and stain the carpet and sofa. I immediately replaced her glass with one that wouldn't break.

Well, I guess some events can't be changed—you can alter events but the outcome is the same. One of the dogs jumped up on her lap and she spilled her red wine on herself and all over the sofa and carpet. But the plastic glass didn't shatter!

Question: You've mentioned on talk radio shows that you can cause lights to go out and affect electricity. Can you give some examples of this?

Answer: Since childhood I've had the ability to cause street lights to go off, as well as rows of ceiling lights at grocery stores and department stores, which my husband can attest to. I don't consciously will the lights to go out, but somehow they do.

During my teen years I conducted an experiment with the fifties Studebaker I wrote about earlier in the book. It was late at night as I drove home on a country road, alone, and decided to steer the car with my thoughts. Remember, this car didn't have power steering, making it difficult to control.

I felt an immense power take over, steering the Studebaker while it remained on the road, without drifting to either side of the highway. This lasted for several minutes until I felt a presence in the back seat and lost control of the car, nearly going into a ditch.

I haven't tried the experiment again. I have learned through the years that I can will things to happen, but I never attempt to control people against their will. I learned that lesson as a child.

Recently my husband, Rick, and I were shopping at Costco. He stood a few feet from me as I pondered over which cheese to purchase. He heard a pop directly above me as one light went out, followed by an entire row of lights. I was oblivious to what had just happened, but suspected something when Rick shook his head and started laughing. This happens all the time, and I'm sure someday

I'll be banned from shopping at those stores.

Not long ago I conducted a little survey on Facebook. At least ten people responded with stories of how they can make street lights to go out as they walk under them. There must be thousands of us with this psi ability. Just think what we could accomplish if we put our minds to it. That's a whole lot of energy to tap into!

Question: I've heard that animals don't have souls. Can you clarify this for me?

Answer: Yes, animals most definitely do have souls, but not like human souls. They also reincarnate. Animals are brilliant, and in many ways much smarter than humans. They are connected to both the physical and spiritual world, and sense when someone or something is going to die or when a disaster is near. Animals know they don't end when they die. Animals move through dimensions.

Animals are more concerned with their surroundings than humans, and can move from one dimension to the next. Also, every living creature dreams, just like humans. They are creating the world they live in, just as humans create the world we exist in today.

Animals are here to teach us valuable lessons, and to hold the vibrational rate of the planet. They hold the vibrational rate of the Earth through their songs, toning and energies.

Realize that there is great intelligence in all life forms.

Many people abuse animals while thinking that their harm does not matter. Any harm or abuse to animals on the planet, anywhere, is recorded on the Akashic Records. All that Creator has created is not to be taken lightly, from the lowest to the highest of animals.

Have you noticed that cats and dogs have individual personalities, just like humans, and that they demonstrate reasoning and intelligence? Have you noticed that your pet is intuitive, knows time, and can read your thoughts? Have you also noticed that they dream, feel emotion, and feel pain?

How could God's creatures not have souls? Animals don't evolve in the same way as humans, but they do evolve and grow. Everything evolves and returns to the God consciousness.

I'll relate my own personal story. I once had a beautiful black and tan hound dog puppy, named Halley. She was so amazing and so smart, but one day she seemed lethargic and sickly.

That night an angelic being appeared in my dream and said, "I must take your dog soon. It's her time to go." I pleaded for the angel to spare my beloved dog, but the angelic woman only smiled and said, "She will be fine."

Days later our veterinarian discovered Halley had a fox tail, a barbed weed, embedded deep within her body, which had traveled to her spine. She stopped eating as her hind legs became paralyzed. There was nothing more that could be done except put Halley down.

The dream told me that animals do cross over into the spirit world with us, and have their own angels and spirit guides. They reincarnate to be with us from lifetime to lifetime.

One of the most amazing videos of animal communication with a black leopard appeared on YouTube. Animal whisper/communicator Anna Breytenbach, of South Africa, has dedicated her life to what she calls 'interspecies communication'. In a video documentary Anna transformed an angry black leopard named Diablo into a relaxed, contented cat.

When Anna arrived at the Jukani Wildlife Sanctuary in South Africa, she was given little information about the angry black leopard. She looked directly into the big cat's eyes, and said that he was awed by his surroundings but stressed by the treatment he received at his prior residence (a zoo). Anna sensed that the animal had been abused and had become wary of humans. He also disliked the dark name Diablo, and asked that his name be changed.

Anna said the big cat commanded respect. He was powerful both physically and in wisdom. Diablo was renamed Spirit, and soon began to explore his new surroundings outside his cage. He became a different cat. This video is proof that animals have great intelligence and wisdom, if we'd only take time to honor them.

To learn more about Anna and her amazing work, visit her website at: www.animalspirit.org

Question: Scientists say that dolphins and whales are more intelligent than humans, but what have these animals done for the world?

Answer: Whales and dolphins tone, creating vibrational sounds that hold our world together. They play a vital part in the planet. Without these highly evolved sea creatures our world would not exist. To destroy them would be to destroy our world.

We can learn to dream with them, and create a new Earth. They are waiting for us to learn this potent lesson, and to heal the planet.

Question: There continues to be a debate about vegetarians verses meat eaters, but who is right?

Answer: Both! Ancient man/woman depended on meat to survive. Indigenous people and ancient people honored the wild food they killed, and realized the godliness in all creatures, so the animal was thanked and blessed for the food it provided. Native American tribes have ceremonies to honor an animal killed for food or a tree cut down for their Sun Dance ceremony. Nothing is taken for granted. Today most cattle, pigs, sheep, and chickens are abused, as videos and news reports indicate. They are fed food, mostly GMO corn, that they would never eat normally, and some are given hormones to fatten them up before the slaughter.

Animals sense their death, releasing the fear hormone in their bodies before they are slaughtered. The consumer then eats the meat containing the fear hormone as well as other toxic substances fed to them. Is it any wonder that humans have so many health problems and cancers from the toxic food we eat?

If the body feels good living on a vegetarian diet, this is great. Others, though, might need some meats, and that's fine too. However, too much red meat is bad for any system, because of the high iron content. If you must eat meat, find animals that are free range, grass fed and treated well.

All creatures that are eaten should be honored for providing food, including fish the way our ancestor and indigenous people have for thousands of years. Anything killed was prayed over and thank for its life. But now creatures are being killed *en masse*, rounded up and slaughtered without any compassion or remorse, like the wild horses in Nevada and dolphins in Japan. Humans must again learn to live in balance with Mother Earth, a living being, and walk in a sacred way upon her. All creatures are sentient beings with intelligence, souls, and they help hold the Earth's grid together by their travels into other realms. They are constantly traveling to other realities and anchoring the grid through their sounds and toning. Without them, life on earth would not exist. Everything is connected to spirit and has a reason for being here.

Question: Is it true that we all astral project into other worlds when we dream, and even see our loved ones who have passed on?

Answer: When we dream our subconscious mind leaves the physical body and is free to roam in the astral world. In a sense, each night that you sleep you enter the death world. When you wake from dream and sense it was real, it was.

Question: Why is there evil?

Answer: There are worlds where evil does not exist. In our duality world evil exists for a purpose. Without evil, how would anyone learn and advance? It's a necessary balance in our world. However, the world is out of balance or *ayni* (pronounced eye-knee) as the indigenous say, and a great correction is about to happen. The Maya, the Hopi and other indigenous elders have predicted that we are going from the fourth world into the fifth world, a time when the Earth will be cleansed of negativity.

As human beings, we seek the impossible—we strive in hardships, and become better people for it. Our world is full of duality; for example, dark and light, hot and cold. Without opposites there is no growth.

Question: In 1984 Ruth Montgomery channeled the book, *Strangers Among Us,* about walk-ins. Do they really exist?

Answer: Absolutely! I've met two "walk-ins" through the years. Both of them claimed one day they woke up and felt their families weren't their families anymore. Their families had become strangers overnight. Nothing seemed right to them. They no longer had the same interests, and no longer shared a connection with families, spouses or friends.

I sense the walk-in phenomenon isn't happening as much now. According to Ruth Montgomery, earthly souls make an agreement with a soul on the Other Side to switch places. This is a mutual agreement between two souls. Walking into an adult body provides the vehicle to complete the soul's mission much faster than incarnating as a baby and going through years to be an adult and accomplish their soul mission.

This is not a spirit possession.

Question: Do demons exist?

Answer: I have never dealt with this, but I believe there are dark entities that reside on lower astral planes of existence. They access our world through portals, and attach themselves to people who have lowered their vibrational frequency through drugs and sometimes alcohol. There are also people who attract these entities because of their misuse of the occult. There are cases where dark forces feed on the mentally ill or innocent children.

Question: Do soul mates exist?

Answer: I prefer "soul friends." We have many soul friends who travel with us in life times for the adventure and spiritual lessons. A soul mate doesn't have to be a husband, or wife, not a sexual relationship. A soul mate can be a sister, friend, brother, neighbor, or even a stranger who helps you along your path. A soul mate is someone you've known in prior lifetimes and who helps you work out karma in this lifetime. A soul mate for eternity is a romantic thought but not a practical one—but don't despair because most of our soul mates are with us lifetime after lifetime. We are like actors on a stage, creating each exciting experience for soul growth. Every soul has the ability to decide on the type of experience they want to play out. It's all a wonderful God-given adventure.

Question: When we first pass over, who greets us on the Other Side?
Answer: It can be a departed relative or friend, and in some cases an angel or spirit guide arrives disguised as a family member, to ease us into our new reality. There are stories of people who have NDEs (near-death experiences) and describe meeting Jesus, Buddha and other spiritually evolved beings. Although I can't confirm or deny their visualization of these beings, I do know that we are all met by highly evolved spiritual beings.

Remember, we are thought forms, pure energy, when we cross over, and we can create whatever we want. I taught my sister that when she died she would become pure energy and could create any reality which would transport her anywhere instantly. Obviously, she learned her lessons well about the Other Side because of her continual validations and visits.

Question: Why must we reincarnate?
Answer: You were given free-will. If you decide you've had enough of Earth, you do not need to return. Your spirit guides help you assess your spiritual growth and your options.

The universe is never ending and expanding. We are the same: never ending, playing out different roles and dramas, learning, growing, evolving and transforming, like caterpillars that change into beautiful butterflies.

Question: If reincarnation really exists, why don't I recall these past lives?

Answer: Can you imagine your brain holding hundreds, even thousands of lifetime memories—of lost loves, children, parents, pain, births, and tragic deaths? It would cause insanity or certainly mess with you mentally and emotionally. Don't we have a difficult enough time living from day to day in our present reality?

Some people, especially children recall past lives until they reach 7 or 8-years-of-age as past life memories slowly fade.

Many people get hints of past lives by the type of music they like, the people they instantly like or dislike, the food they eat, the places they like to visit or hope to visit, unexplained phobias, hobbies like collecting Civil War guns. Even our dreams can provide hints to past lives. I had a recurring dream of ancient catacombs somewhere in the Holy land, but that's all I remember. I've also experienced glimpses of a past lives in the old West and ancient Egypt.

Question: Are past lives relevant to this life?

Answer: Absolutely! On occasion, healing and lessons need to take place from events that happened in past lives. Dr. Brian Weiss, an American psychiatrist and New York bestselling author, was astonished and skeptical when one of his patients began recalling past-life traumas that seemed to hold the key to her recurring nightmares and anxiety attacks. His skepticism was eroded, however, when she began to channel messages from "the space between lives," which contained remarkable revelations about Dr. Weiss's family and his dead son. Using past-life therapy, he was able to cure the patient and embark on a new, more meaningful phase of his own career.

Dr. Brian Weiss first book was, *Many Lives, Many Master,* an excellent book on reincarnation followed by six more books on the subject. I highly recommend his books.

Question: Who determines what sex we are born into?

Answer: It depends on what is needed for our soul growth. Our guides and council help us select the roles we will take in the new incarnations. The major reason we return is for soul growth and to learn unconditional love. Because we are able to forget who we were in the past, this makes it so much easier to learn things on a deeper level and expand even more from it. If humanity learned that we were created by the same God force, there would be more tolerance, more love, and more compassion for one another. We would see the divine spark in all living creatures and honor that spark. Most souls decide on the same sex they were in a prior lifetime.

Question: Is my life destined by the stars?

Answer: Only you map out your life, not the stars, not fate, not destiny. Astrology is a road map to follow and guide you on your soul path. You were given special gifts when you were born on a certain day, year, time and place. That star map doesn't control your life, you do! You are the master and creator of your life path.

But remember that fear is a magnet and what you fear, you create. An example of fear creating reality is actress Natalie Wood, who was deathly afraid of dark water. She drowned in the Pacific Ocean on November 29, 1981, while on a boating trip near Santa Catalina Island with her husband Robert Wagner and actor Christopher Walken.

We can also create a beautiful life with positive thoughts. Manifestation is our birth right.

Question: There are books on the Crystalline, Indigo, New Children, Star Children, and Rainbow Children born in the last fifteen years. Who are these children and why have they arrived?

Answer: In the last twenty years a large number of children have come into the world with special gifts and talents that are beyond normal. They are supernatural children, who remember where they existed before birth and recall past lives. They see and communicate with spirits; they possess telepathic, telekinetic and psychic gifts as well innate talents that make them prodigies in healing, the arts, science, mathematics, music, and writing.

Doctors often mislabel the new children as autistic, ADD, ADHD, or suggest other behavioral difficulties, but what they don't understand is these children are vibrating on a higher frequency, with changed DNA.

More than half the time, these doctors are wrong. The new children are not defective. Unfortunately, many of these children have gone unnoticed and appreciated by the world. Some of these special children have made themselves known by changing the world through creating charities that stop starvation in third world countries and help build schools for their education. One such charity is Free the Children at www.freethechildren.com. The charity began in 1995 when Craig Kielburger gathered 11 school friends to begin fighting child labor. He was 12.

I have met many of the new children, and know they have arrived to change the world through their higher vibrations. They offer us hope for an improved world. Suggested books: *The Children of Now* by Meg Blackburn Losey, Ph.D. and *The Indigo Children* by Lee Carroll.

For seniors in the world, you are the Golden Indigos born during the 40s, 50s, and 60s who paved the way for the evolved new children that began coming in to the Earth's plane during the 1980s.

Question: Lately I've seen orb photos posted everywhere on the internet. What are they?

Answer: Orbs are pure intelligence. I have photographed them, and have friends who have captured some remarkable photographs of them moving, which leave a streak across the photograph. My dear friend Diane, in New York State, is constantly capturing strange and beautiful orbs, both at night and during the day. She has a connection to these beings. In some cases a camera catches light from different sources and creates an orb photograph. I've photographed snow falling where orbs appear, and I believe the flash from the camera on the snowflakes created the orbs—nothing paranormal.

Orbs have been seen where crop circles are formed, where they have been seen in the sky, and the three children of Fatima, Portugal, in 1917, watched an orb float in from the east, and materialize into a Marian apparition. Orbs have also been photographed in cemeteries. Ghostly orbs are caught on camera by ghost hunters for various TV shows, and can be quite photogenic when they want to be. Even TLC's Long island Medium Theresa Caputo featured a client who captured an orb on her cell phone as it bounced around her house. Theresa sensed it was the woman's deceased child.

One of the more interesting accounts of orbs is in Dr. Meg Blackburn Losey's book, *The Children of Now,* where Dr. Losey described living children who have connected with her in orb form. At first she thought it was her imagination, but she has learned that the phenomenon is real. She wrote that she found a group of children who communicate telepathically, and there is a small group she calls the "Beautiful Silent Ones." They are the amazing children who, at a glance, appear to be considerably less than perfect, in fact nonfunctional, with severe disabilities, at least on the outside. Many have autism. They are the Crystalline, or Children of the Stars, but they are most definitely here with evolutionary energetic patterns.

Dr. Losey believes these children are the forerunners of the new evolution of humanity—they are the thousands of "new" children arriving now.

So orbs are intelligence in many forms, here to awaken our consciousness. They are deceased souls, celestial beings, dimensional beings, angels, and living children.

Question: You have written about your UFO experiences and perhaps an alien encounter in your book, *Angels, Aliens and Prophecy II,* but can you tell me why are they here?

Answer: Since childhood I've known that life is everywhere, and that intelligence beings watch us. I believe we are about to awaken *en masse* to other realities and dimensional beings soon. I believe they are here to help us on our evolutionary path. There are many species of beings watching us, and like humans, some of them are highly evolved spiritually, and others aren't and have less than positive agenda for humanity.

I recently had the opportunity to interview Ron Felber about his book *Searchers: The True Story of Alien Abduction,* based on the true account of a young couple, Steve and Dawn, from Southern California, who were held hostage in 1989 by alien beings for twelve hours in the Mojave Desert of California.

This is one of the most believable alien abductions I've ever read. Steve and Dawn agreed to hypnosis to uncover more of their alien abduction story, and this is what they revealed:

"The aliens want to make contact with us. They were sent on missions throughout the universe by the One Supreme."

A question asked of Dawn: "You talked about the universe and matter earlier. You said, 'Our universe ends where theirs begins…'"

Dawn answered, "Our universe ends when its matter stops mattering to us and starts mattering to them." Dawn also said these beings would intervene into our world if war or mass destruction seemed imminent.

When asked what the One Supreme asks of us, the reply was, "For all the galaxies to live harmoniously together."

And so I leave you to contemplate that grand concept!

Question: I've heard stories of how spirits have saved lives? Can you relate any story about that?

Answer: Here's a miracle story that happened recently. Jennifer Grosbeck, a 25-year-old mother was returning home with her 18-

month-old baby, Lily, after visiting her parents on March 6. Something caused Jennifer's car to go off the side of the road and plunge in the river near Spanish Fork, Utah. The car was turned upside down in the river. Fourteen hours later a fisherman happened to be in the area and spotted the hidden car under the bridge and called authorities. Four police officers arrived at the scene and heard a distinct female voice from the car saying, "help me, help us," and that is when we said, "We're trying to help you. We're trying our best to get you out." The voice was clear as day," said Spanish Fork police officer Tyler Beddoes. That mysterious female voice increased the policemen's adrenaline which enabled them to pull the heavy, water-logged car onto its side. That's when they found the mother dead at the wheel, but her 18-month-old baby was still miraculously alive strapped her infant seat upside down. Lily had somehow survived 14 hours, in temperatures that dipped to as low as 20 degrees Fahrenheit.

What makes this story so incredible is the mother died on impact, so how did they police officers hear a voice? Was it the mother or spiritual guides/angels? Knowing how a mother's instinct is to save her child, I have no doubt that Jennifer was there with her daughter all night. Not even death could stop Jennifer from saving her baby.

All seven emergency responders had to be hospitalized and treated for hypothermia after being in the very cold river, yet Lily survived 14 hours in the cold. Although in critical condition, she has now been released from the hospital and is doing very well with her father. I'd say Lily has an important mission in this world.

Question: Is there time travel, and can we manipulate time?

Answer: In my book, *Angels, Aliens and Prophecy II*, time I discussed time travel, but will go into it as much as I understand it. Quantum physicists believe time travel is possible. There have been many experiments, such as the double-slit experiment, or Young's experiment, where electrons and protons were fired into a panel with two slits. What appeared on the panel were three smudges, which baffled scientists. Something strange and unknown was taking place.

Here's another time anomaly that would blow Doc Brown's mind from the movie *Back to the Future*. Scientists discovered that if you want a time warp simple walk up some stairs. It turns out that time isn't the same all over; it actually runs faster in higher places. In another experiment scientists placed two atomic clocks on two tables, then raised one of the tables by 33 centimeters and found out that the higher clock was running faster than the lower one at a rate of 90-billionth of a second in 79 years. This is called time dilation, and it happens because (as Einstein's theory of relativity predicted) gravity warps time as well as space.

There are stories of time travel and time slips where people from this time period suddenly find themselves propelled in another era, usually from the past. This might explain the mysterious disappearances of people, ships, planes and boats.

Time is a construct. All time is simultaneous. A planet has layers of energy grids around it that allows it to be experienced from its various time frames. Earth has many portals where beings can enter into our reality.

Some of these time portals exist in the Mexico/Central

America area, California's Mount Shasta, the Mideast, Easter Island, Mount Fuji, Lake Titicaca, the Nazca lines in Peru, Uluru (or Ayers) Rock in Australia, and the Bermuda Triangle. There is also one in the Sinai, and there is one over Tibet. These are some of the major portals through which energies arrive and depart on our planet.

There are those highly evolved people on Earth, like Tibetan monks, who can access these portals and peer into the future. This is how they prepared for the invasion of Tibet by the Chinese. They took valuable artifacts and ancient texts to be hidden as they fled Tibet for India to go into exile. This is how His Holiness The Dalai Lama survived the invasion of Tibet. The Tibetan Oracle had foreseen the invasion of Tibet by the Chinese long before it happened.

Time lines can be changed by creating a Prime Event, such as the Harmonic Convergence in 1987, organized by Dr. Jose Arguelles. Millions of people heard about this event and gathered in meditation and prayer on August 16-17, 1987. Through their prayers the Berlin Wall eventually came down in 1989.

Another time line change happened on 9-11 in 2001. Our world was altered on that day. In order to anchor a new time line onto the planet, there has to be a mass event that takes place.
The Harmonic Convergence was created from a future time line and set into the present. What created this event? The mass consciousness of people, uniting in love and peace.

I truly believe and have been told by spirit that we can change events and time lines when humanity unites in a common benevolent goal. We are the masters of our fate, and the sooner we awaken to this fact, the sooner our planet will be healed, and peace will envelop the world.

***Question*:** Have you ever had a spirit come through during a talk show interview?

Answer: Several times, but in 2013 I was invited on BTR talk radio show with host Java Bob. Before the show he mentioned his young daughter had passed away the year before. In fact, it was the anniversary of her passing the night of my interview. During the interview I kept hearing a small child's voice whisper repeatedly, "Babba Jav! Babba Jav!" The voice was persistent, yet playful.

I couldn't get the voice out of my head through the entire interview and knew a child had a message for Bob. Finally I felt compelled to say something on air. "Did your daughter have a funny pet name for you, like Babba Jav?"

There was a long silence and then he laughed, "She did, in fact, call me Babba Jav. How incredible you picked that up tonight."

I was honored to have validated his daughter's love from the Other Side.

Chapter Seventeen
Kathy's Big Surprise

It had been a while since Kathy's last visitation, and my husband Rick and I believed the activity was over. Oh boy, were we in for a surprise. Kathy's next visit took place on May 18, 2014.

Usually on Sunday morning Rick and I watch CBS's Sunday Morning show. One this particular day a segment featured a story on "Happy or Smiley Faces" and how people always use them on emails and on Facebook. The classic smiley face design first appeared in 1963, comprised of a yellow circle with two black dots (representing eyes) and a black arc (representing the mouth). It is sometimes used as a generic term for any emoticon. At breakfast we discussed the show further, and how my husband gets lots of emails from his clients with "Happy Faces."

Later that morning, while I worked in my office, I heard Rick in his office let out a yelp. In a flash he stood at my office door holding a coaster he used for his water glass. On it was a perfect water-marked "Happy Face."

Kathy's Happy Face on coaster

No doubt Kathy had listened to our conversation, and decided to get the last laugh. So, if you doubt that our departed loved ones don't have a sense of humor, think again!

The activity returned on Memorial Day, May 26, the day I was scheduled to return on Coast to Coast AM talk radio show with George Noory, at eleven pm Pacific Time. At seven in the morning our radio shut off, and again at 9:30 am. At first I thought Kathy was there for the holiday, but I sensed she had more on her mind. Kathy wanted me to capture her image on video, so at 10 am I set up my laptop and told Kathy about my experiment. As soon as I walked into the dining room and stood next to the stereo, the radio shut off. I asked Kathy to appear in the video, turned on my video camera, and left the room for thirty minutes. What I captured shows an orb and an image walking forward and backward on the front of the stereo. This is now posted on YouTube, and on my website www.betseylewis.com under Media.

What appeared on the video was stunning. Remember when I told you how I convinced Kathy to walk backwards for a day because I thought it would change her destiny? I have no doubt she wanted to remind me of the incident by walking forward and then backward, and believe me, I got her message loud and clear.

Whenever I think Kathy is gone, I always get a clear message from her. Recently on what would have been her birthday, February 24, our stereo-radio began turning off every five minutes. That night I said a silent prayer to Kathy, telling her that I loved her, but it was all right for her to move on. For the next seven days the radio stayed on--no sign from Kathy. I told my husband about my prayer to Kathy, and he believed she wasn't ready to leave because of all the activity.

Boy, did I have another surprise on the eighth day. It was morning as the Kool Oldies Radio station played hits from the sixties and seventies and as I had walked out of the room and returned The Jackson Five sang, *Never Can Say Goodbye, Girl,* and the radio instantly shut off by itself. My husband burst into laughter and said, "Guess she told you. She's never leaving!"

If you still don't believe that spirits can communicate with the living, then nothing will convince you that life goes on after death, and that we are more alive on the Other Side than in our physical reality. I can tell you one thing, if you're a gambler; the odds of such things happening are astronomical. One thing I'm certain of is this—when it's my time to pass over to the Other Side, Kathy will be waiting for me with open arms, wearing her "Happy Face," and that will be a glorious day.

Epilogue

Ancient humans didn't possess computers, television, cell phones, or other modern technology to warn them of hurricanes, tornadoes, floods, erupting volcanoes, warring tribes or dangerous animal predators. Instead, ancient humans survived by using their instincts and sixth sense.

Unfortunately, in the last 200 years, humans have used less of their sixth sense, due to modern technology and instant news. My psychic abilities are not unique, and the same goes for famous mediums like Theresa Caputo, John Edward, James Van Praagh, and Patrick Mathews. Each and every one of us has psychic potential to communicate with spirits and to foresee the future.

We have forgotten how to trust our intuition—that feeling, or little voice inside, that warns us not to cross the street, or get on a plane that will eventually crash, or stay away from the beach when a tsunami hits hours later. There are countless stories of people who have been saved by their intuition and their guardian angels/spirit guides.

We live in amazing and wondrous times. Since childhood I've been shown massive earth changes in recurring dreams, and I believe we are now in those times. In the past few years we've seen disaster after disaster from unprecedented extreme weather, winds, tornadoes, hurricanes, flash floods, droughts, sinkholes, and wildfires. Some of the strangest things happening globally are the booms heard everywhere. Mother Earth is going through a physical shift, as well as a magnetic pole shift. The booms are created as the Earth is stretched and pulled apart in the stretch zones and tectonic fault areas, when the air above those areas slaps together. This will increase in the coming months. We'll see more meteors, as well as large asteroids flying past Earth. There will be more sea creatures dying *en masse* as methane gas escapes from vents deep in the oceans around the world.

Will governments tell us the truth that our planet is going to shift? Never! I believe Planet X, also known as Nibiru, a brown dwarf, or failed, star, travels through our solar system every 3,700 years. So far astrophysicists have discovered most solar systems have binary stars or revolve around a common centre mass. Our solar system is the exception, or is it? This might explain Planet X's existence in our solar system, if it does exist.

There are theories that Planet X is currently traveling through our solar system. Its magnetic pull on Earth is greater than the sun's pull, which is causing deep core Earth movement. Other planets have been displaying anomalies in the past few years, and this will continue.

According to sources like Zeta contactee Nancy Lieder, the

Earth is tilted at an angle. Earth's wobble is such that when the magnetic North Pole of Earth comes over the horizon the globe gets a polar push, pushing the N Pole of Earth away to avoid the blast from the N Pole of Planet X. This is when the Sun is high over the Pacific, or dawn in Australia. Thus as Australia is moving North at that time, the Sun overhead seems to be curving too far to the South. Those familiar with these mechanics know they can check with a planetarium program such as Skymap to ascertain the expected angle of the Ecliptic from any place, at any time.

In the BBC documentary that first aired June 18, 2012, now available on YouTube, it showed a live government webcam stationed at an Antarctica weather station. The live webcam recorded video every fifteen minutes. What was so startling was around July 14, 2011, when the sun is no longer visible in the Antarctic, something brilliant light up the station in total darkness. Planet X does not have its own light source, but reflects light from the sun.

Indigenous people of the Arctic region who live outdoors and observe nature, the sun, the stars, the wind, have noticed strange and disturbing changes in the sun in the last few years. Elder Ludy Pudluk of Resolute Bay said he has noticed big changes the way the sun sets. It's as if the earth tilted on its axis. They say the sun is higher, warmer, and the stars look different, and not in their proper positions. There is no longer a north wind, but a dominant east wind.

Earth is going to experience a major upheaval as she has for thousands of years, to evolve and cleanse herself of man-made toxins. In order for us and the planet to survive, this event (which I have dreamed about since the age of 7) is going to happen in our lifetime. A new world is coming, and with the new world we will evolve spiritually.

It's obvious that a great number of us are realizing we made an agreement before we came into our physical bodies that we would come together at a certain time in order to bring in the light and love onto planet Earth and to usher in a Golden Age. Some have forgotten while others have a strange feeling, like a lost-dream, that we have mission to accomplish before our planet shifts. We are all experiencing a movement, a Shift, and wanting to change, knowing our planet can't continue in the old paradigm.

There are over 7.2 billion of us being asked to help raise the planet's vibrational rate, and realize we have the power to do it. Currently, we are out of balance, but once we remember our part in raising Earth's vibrational rate, we will help the Golden Age become reality.

In order to survive these coming planetary changes, we must trust our intuition, trust the animals who sense geomagnetic changes, pets included, and get back to honoring our precious planet Earth through prayers, intention, meditation and ceremony, like the indigenous peoples have done for thousands of years. As Earth changes increase (and I know they will), it's imperative to trust our sixth sense, and trust Mother Earth and the animals to warn us.

Begin by visiting nature, and observing everything and nature's aliveness. Mother Earth always warns us before natural disasters, but we seldom listen. A good example of this: wild creatures and domestic animals can sense or hear changes before earthquakes strike. It is believed that animals sense the geomagnetic changes taking place in the planet.

Just before a 9.3 magnitude earthquake struck Indonesia on December 26, 2004, animals and birds began leaving the coastal areas for higher ground. Tourists and locals watched as the ocean receded out of bays, and ran into the bay to observe the strange phenomenon. Moments later, a tsunami, 98' feet tall, came roaring back along the coasts of fourteen countries. It is estimated over 500,000 people died that day. Had those people trusted their intuition and followed the animals to higher ground, most would have survived.

As spiritual leader of the Western Shoshone Nation Corbin Harney said, "We redskin people have a chance to survive because we're connected to what's out there. We can talk to a lot of things. We can ask water to continue to flow and be purer and cleaner water for us. The Creator listens to us if we talk to him.

"We have to come back to the Native way of life. The Native way is to pray for everything. Our Mother Earth is very important. We can't just misuse her and think she's going to continue. I've seen a lot of visions, but I don't like to talk about them, because generally nobody believes in what I'm saying. There are visions among all of us, not only Indian people; white men also have visions."

Corbin knew spirit was in everything and said, "The Spirit tells the people what to get, where to go. Today we think, well, it's just luck if something good happens. It's not luck. It's the Spirit telling us, guiding us all the way!"

He reminded us of our visions, and said, "Some of us understand what a vision is, even though it's something that everybody has. All the living things on this planet of ours, everything has a vision. Even the planet itself has a vision, and now it's beginning to warn us that something's going to become different pretty quick, if we don't do something about it. This kind of vision is given from the Earth to the people, but the people aren't paying attention to the visions. We think they're just something that we've dreamed up, or something that we just don't understand."

Global mass consciousness can change human-created and natural events. Although, with natural disasters, we may not change the event, but I believe we can lessen its severity. First of all we must unite in a common, benevolent quest. At the moment everything is out of ayni—out of balance. When we discover that we're dreaming the world into existence, and we realize that we also create the nightmares, there will be balance again.

We are living in a very interesting time where many truths that were once hidden are coming to light, and there will be much more in the coming years. Mother Earth, like us, is evolving and changing, and she needs our prayers and love more than ever. I envision a future Earth where we live in harmony with the planet and all living creatures, where we honor the spiritual world, and where humans use their psychic powers daily—telepathy, telekinesis, and the precognitive ability. Can you imagine a world where everyone is telepathic and can read each other's thoughts? There would be no more lies or secrets— only truth!

Grandmother Clara of the Amazon, was one of the 13 Indigenous Grandmothers of the world who gathered in Phoenicia, New York from October 11 through October 17, 2004, and told of the time she was visited by the Star Beings who confirmed that

December 21, 2012 heralded the "Galactic Dawn"—a mass awakening of humanity to our cosmic origins and the intergalactic relationships. But this was just the beginning for humanity in a grand awakening that is still taking place when we finally realize that everything has consciousness and we are connected to all things. The day we honor Mother Earth, the oceans, waters, finned ones, winged ones, and the animals as sentient beings, door that have been closed to us for eons will suddenly open again to other worlds and dimension. What a day that will be!

The Lakota Sioux have a saying, *Mitakuye Oyasin*, which means *we are all related*! As astrophysicist, Neil deGrasse Tyson reminds us, *the atoms of our bodies are traceable to stars that manufactured them in their cores and exploded these enriched ingredients across our galaxy, billions of years ago. For this reason, we are biologically connected to every other living thing in the world. We are chemically connected to all molecules on Earth. And we are atomically connected to all atoms in the universe. We are not figuratively, but literally STARDUST.*

About Betsey Lewis

Betsey Lewis, an internationally-renowned psychic/medium, talk show host of Rainbow Vision Network and earth mysteries investigator, inherited the gift of prophecy from her mother.

For over forty years Betsey has investigated UFO sightings, cattle mutilations, angels, aliens, and other Earth mysteries. She practices Reiki, Kriya Yoga, astrology, tarot and numerology, and regressive hypnosis. She spent ten years with Native American ceremonial and spiritual leaders, learning Earthkeeper ways through pow-wows, healing ceremonies, vision quests, and sweat lodge ceremonies in the Western U.S., Canada and Central America.

Betsey has hosted the Rainbow Vision Network since 2009, featuring bestselling authors and renowned investigators into the paranormal and metaphysical world. She has been a guest on Fox Channel's The Dr. Michael Show, Idaho's KTVB Noon show, KIVI Morning show, and numerous radio talk shows including Coast to Coast AM with George Noory, KTALK's The Fringe, X-Zone, and Ground Zero Talk Radio. Betsey was a keynote speaker at the 2012 UFO Conference in Alamo, Nevada, near Area 51.

Published nonfiction books include: *Never Can Say*

Goodbye—Answers to Life's Greatest Mysteries, Mystic Revelations of Thirteen—The Key to Earth's Destiny; Angels, Aliens and Prophecy—The Connection, Angels, Aliens and Prophecy II—The Angel-Alien Agenda, Earth Energy—Return to Ancient Wisdom and three spiritual books for young adults and children—*Alexander Phoenix and The Seven Sacred Virtues*, *The Story of Rainbow Eyes*, and *A Worm Named Sherm*.

Betsey lives in Southwestern Idaho with her husband and her two beloved pets, a dog and cat. Betsey's website: www.betseylewis.com . She maintains her popular Earth News1 blog on her website.

Made in the USA
San Bernardino, CA
07 October 2016